Wicked Solutions

A Systems Approach to Complex Problems

Bob Williams and Sjon van 't Hof

A workbook

Published by Bob Williams

ISBN 978-1-326-51229-3

First published 2014

Second edition 2016

Two 30 minute videos covering the contents of this book are available to view here:
https://www.youtube.com/watch?v=lFcWhGE7moQ and
https://www.youtube.com/watch?v=5RRHpXl2hrw
They are edited highlights of a workshop run in 2015 by Bob Williams at the Research
Institute for Humanity and the Environment in Kyoto.

Front cover design: BoJe@nne (See also fig. 4.2 at the end of section 'Wicked Solutions')
Photos and tables: authors, except indicated otherwise
Concept maps: Sjon van 't Hof

Table of Contents

What is this book about?

Every noble act is at first impossible.

Thomas Carlisle

It's not worth doing something unless you were doing something that someone, somewhere, would much rather you weren't doing.

Terry Pratchett

This book is about the use of core systems ideas in dealing with wicked situations. Wicked situations are those where identifying problems is not easy and selecting good solutions is even more difficult. Many societal, business and development challenges are in fact wicked problems.

Using three basic systems concepts, **inter-relationships**, **perspectives** and **boundaries**, this book will help you:

- assess wicked situations

- unpick the tangle of issues that need addressing

- design suitable ways of tackling those issues

- deal with some tricky aspects of working in wicked situations

- find more information about systems methods and managing interventions systemically

It is a *Workbook:* We guide you through the steps and stages of a process that addresses your own wicked problem. The locations of the tasks are highlighted in the margin of the text using the TEAMWORK icon. That doesn't mean you have to work with others, but it will help a lot if you do.

TEAMWORK

It is a *Primer:* We introduce you to some core systems ideas and suggest where you can find more information.

It is a *Learning tool:* Not only do we introduce you to a particular way of addressing wicked problems, but explain the rationale so that you can adapt the approach to your own circumstances.

We make no apologies that you might find some parts of the book difficult. We have tried to be as simple as possible but no simpler. You are, after all, dealing with difficult, 'wicked' issues and if there was an easy way to do it then you wouldn't be reading this book. Persevere. You will be glad you did.

Is this book for you?

Are you wrestling with a wicked problem? If you are, then it could be useful to you. Some examples:

- **entrepreneurs** and **managers** who want to secure their business in a sustainable manner by reconciling, e.g., clients' needs, employees' interests and environmental concerns;

- **researchers**, especially **action researchers**, seeking out new tools for inquiry and analysis;

- **teachers** and **lecturers** trying to teach their students how to think and learn about addressing and resolving 'wicked problems' in society and beyond;

- people in networks or **platform organisations,** especially those who work between **public sector**, **private sector** and **civil society** and need to conceive effective ways for communication and collaboration;

- **policy workers** who are trying to explore the consequences of adopting various strategies and tactics;

- **evaluators** called upon to help people assess the value of interventions that are clearly very messy with lots of possible ways of judging worth;

- **consultants** and **coaches** who want to demonstrate that systems thinking leads to more sustainable results;

- **community workers** trying to steer projects along complicated paths in difficult environments.

Apart from these professionals, this book may also prove useful to students in secondary and tertiary education, politicians, reporters and interested members of the general public.

The book in a nutshell

The core of this book deals with the systemic design of interventions to address wicked problems. Wicked problems are systemic problems that are characterised by multiple stakeholders involved in complex and unpredictable interactions. Stakeholders are people or organisations with an interest in the (wicked) problem and its (re-)solution. Systemically designed interventions are needed because conventional understanding and management cannot address wicked problems.

Systemic design is able to take into account the complex inter-relationships and divergent perspectives of the key stakeholders and use this information in a clever way to design an effective intervention by deliberating critical issues. These issues are related to the purpose, resources, knowledge and legitimacy of the intervention. They are also known as boundary issues and the deliberation of these critical issues is also known as *boundary critique*. A key goal of the critique is to warrant whether the purpose is attained, the right resources are under control, the knowledge is appropriate and the intervention as a whole is legitimate.

The boundary critique does not stop there. A technique aimed at *stakeholding development* is used to explore the practical design limits from both a positive and a more conservative point of view. This is followed by a method that combines the best of both the actual and the ideal world into a realistic intervention design. After that you can use regular planning methods or other systems methods to improve or finalise your intervention design.

While we have tried to keep this book as short as possible, you may still not manage to drill all the way down to the back cover. You may not even need to. You may just need a gentle push to get on your way. Consequently, this book provides you with three levels by which you can address your wicked problem. Each level takes you deeper and is more thorough than the previous one. You may need that thoroughness, or you may not. Level One, which introduces our inter-relationships, perspectives and boundaries approach, may be just what you need to get started. If it doesn't, then proceed to Level Two, which explores the ideas of inter-relationships, perspectives and boundaries by posing 12 questions. It also acts as a warm-up for Level Three — the full-on forensic approach to exploring wicked problems and developing wicked solutions.

The three levels in this book

LEVEL 1 : GETTING STARTED

Introduces key concepts and
gets you started without much ado

LEVEL 2 : CORE CONCEPTS

Uses 12 key questions to provide
you with further guidance

LEVEL 3 : THE DEEP DIVE

The full works that takes you in 10 steps
from systemic inquiry to intervention design

LEVEL ONE

Getting started

Working with wicked situations

A man who carries a cat by the tail learns something he can learn in no other way.

Mark Twain

There's something, well, wicked about the word wicked. It implies something that's not exactly good but not totally bad either. There's a bit of a challenge but nothing disastrous. A hint of fun and perhaps something a little mysterious or magical. And a promise of resolution. A wave of the wand and things might just sort themselves out. There are many definitions of what elements comprise a wicked problem, but they essentially boil down to these six[1].

- Every wicked problem is novel or unique
- There is a no stopping rule; you can't hit the pause button
- The problem is not understood until the formulation of the solution
- Wicked problems are complex; they have no single cause, no single effect and have no given alternative solution
- Every wicked solution is a 'one shot operation'; there is no off-the-peg 'best practice' answer
- Solutions are not right or wrong, but they may be better or worse.

Wicked problems or wicked situations pose a whole raft of questions. Is the problem or situation unusual or common? Is it resolvable? If so, how? Can anyone help me? Where are they? Many books give you guidance — often very good guidance on addressing those wicked problems. In which case, what is this book's particular contribution?

This book doesn't replace other writings; rather it focuses on a critically important question that often goes unanswered: "Where do I start?"

There are two common reactions when faced with wicked, complicated or complex situations — or, using systems language, a *problématique* or a systems mess (yes, 'mess' is a common systems term). One is blank incomprehension; like a deer in car headlights you are frozen into immobility. The other is to jump in and just, well, start. Neither is especially satisfactory. Freeze, and you just get hit by the situation. Jumping in creates potentially more problems, since a wicked situation will respond to your intervention. To use some more systems jargon, messy, complex situations are starting point sensitive; where you start will determine where you end up. Start anywhere and you may end up nowhere. So the very place to start is to pause, think, deliberate and carefully consider your investigation or intervention. Just because a situation is complex, just because it is not easily controllable doesn't mean that you can't craft your intervention carefully. It doesn't mean anything goes. It doesn't mean things may just come out in the wash. Deliberation may delay action by a few hours or even a few weeks, but unless triage is needed to stop blood flow draining away the life of the situation, careful consideration of where and how to start can save time, lives and expensively acquired resources — like people.

---

[1] Wicked problems comprise a whole field of study of its own. They were first recognised as such by Rittel and Webber in the mid-1960s. They described them in their article Dilemmas in a general theory of planning. C. West Churchman, whose ideas are covered extensively later in this book, is sometimes credited with the term. These were identified by Professor Brian Collins. 23rd INCOSE International Symposium (2013). https://www.youtube..com/watch?v=5JVkj6PvjiQ Retrieved April 2014. Collins's list is similar to that in Chapter 1 of Dialogue Mapping: Building Shared Understanding of Wicked Problems (Conklin, 2005). Chapter 1 is available at http://cognexus.org/wpf/wickedproblems.pdf (retrieved January 2016).

So this is a book that will help you design an inquiry and intervention in messy, wicked situations. However, this isn't a book that regards design as something you do just at the start and then leave fixed, a plan once arrived at that you slavishly follow through. Wicked situations evolve and your intervention needs to be informed by and respond to that evolution. **So the principles and tools in this book should be used throughout your intervention, in a process of intermittent or even constant redesign.**

Thinking systemically: a very short introduction

There are many approaches to thinking systemically, and this book draws on an approach that people who we've worked with all over the world tell us they find helpful. This approach comprises three main building blocks:

Inter-relationships

How do specific items within a situation connect with each other? With what implications for whom? These items can be people, things, ideas and resources, such as money, time, objects, knowledge. In systems language you will often see these called 'agents'.

Perspectives

The systems thinker C. West Churchman famously said: *The systems approach begins when first you see the world through the eyes of another.*

What are the different ways in which a particular situation can be understood? How do perspectives influence how people make sense of that situation? How does it affect their behaviour in a situation? Later in this book you will come across references to a specific way of handling perspectives called 'framing'.

> **Tip to use this book effectively**
>
> The best way to address a complex situation is not noodling on your tablet or computer but systemically working with other people. Why do you think that is? It is not easy to explore situations from radically different perspectives on your own. Bring one other person into the discussion and you'll be surprised at the many perspectives you never thought of. It gets even better with more people and better still if those people come from radically different, even, indeed especially, opposing standpoints.

Boundaries

Our understanding of any situation will always be limited. The possible range of responses to a situation will similarly be restricted by knowledge, resources, our perspectives, our motivations and our priorities. We set boundaries around everything we do; no task can be truly 'holistic' and at some stage we have to make a conscious or unconscious decision about what to leave in and what to leave out. And put simply that's what boundaries do — delineate between what is 'in' (e.g., important, relevant, good, included) and what is 'out' (e.g., unimportant, irrelevant, bad, excluded). But how do you make those decisions? How responsible should we feel for the consequences of our boundary choices? Thus, our choices have ethical, political and practical implications. To quote Churchman again: *Who is embraced by the action area and thus benefits? Who is out and does not benefit? What are the possible consequences of this? And, how might we feel about that?*

Three key concepts

Inter-relationships	– How do things connect with each other?
Perspectives	– What are the different ways a situation can be understood?
Boundaries	– What's 'in' and what's 'out'?

So for us, the core of systems thinking is the application of these three concepts applied together:

An understanding of **inter-relationships**, and

An acknowledgement that multiple **perspectives** inform that understanding, and

Acceptance that **boundary** choices are not optional, but require deliberation for ethical, political and practical reasons.

Level Two of this book looks at these three concepts in much more detail, indeed it is the foundation of this book. But before you dive into deeper water we want to give you a bit of a warm-up. The concepts of inter-relationships, perspectives and boundaries are quite powerful on their own without any of the embellishments that this book adds. In fact, we've known people to get substantial insights on a situation just by playing around with these three concepts.

Here's an example (see also table 1 overleaf):

An international donor agency instigated a project designed to create leadership within a particular scientific field in North Africa. Leadership is a wicked issue — a very dangerous one since many people think that leadership is primarily about people in senior positions who are charismatic champions of a cause. But that sweeps in both heroes and despots. In reality we judge leadership more in terms of what it does than what it is; leadership goes beyond the characteristics of individual leaders. At this point, issues of culture, ego, money, timing and reputation start being incorporated and things get messy — wicked even.

Which is pretty much what the donor agency discovered. The first three phases of their work building leadership in this scientific endeavour were difficult, and understanding the reasons for this was critical to inform future phases of work. The initial three phases were:

1. Funding a single organisation to promote leadership within the field
2. Bringing in other networks of researchers and research institutions to develop collective leadership
3. Establishing a core group drawn from these networks able to exercise a leadership function.

The project officer of the donor agency used the inter-relationships, perspectives and boundaries framework to explore these issues. Her thoughts are described briefly in the following table.

Phases	Inter-relationships *How do things connect with each other?*	Perspectives *What are the different ways a situation can be understood?*	Boundaries *What's in and what's out?*
Phase One **Funding a single organisation to promote leadership within the field**	Mainly donor-funded; few generated spontaneously by the funded organisation, which rather defeated the object of building leadership.	The funder organisation took a specific *leadership* perspective in funding this project. However, the concept of having a project solely dedicated to building leadership was hard to understand by those working in the research field who perceived this primarily from a research perspective not leadership perspective; they were physical scientists not management consultants. So it was unclear what perspective drove this phase.	Only the funded organisation and the donor were included in the critical boundary decisions; which again rather worked against the idea of leadership. What was the funded organisation expected to lead? Who was supposed to benefit from this leadership and how?
Phase Two **Bringing in other networks**	The funder expanded its relationships with a whole range of actors and external stakeholders in this leadership project. This created confusion over who was in charge of the project. The politics of the project became complicated because the project started interfering with existing relationships between actors and rumours that leadership roles were being forced on those actors.	Many other perspectives emerged. The benefits of 'leadership' varied depending on these different perspectives. Some fence-sitting and/or competitive dynamics between various stakeholders was based on their different perspectives on what they thought the project was really about. Was it something to do with leadership, something to do with research, something to do with networking?	The boundary of activity expands, yet the basis for working out who was 'in' the network and who was 'out' of the network wasn't clear. Nor were there clear definitions of 'field' and 'leadership', which again created confusion about who or what was intended to benefit from this intervention.
Phase Three **Establishing a Regional Core Group**	In an attempt to settle inter-relationship issues down, a core group of seven members representing a range of stakeholders was developed. But although there was emerging individual commitment to the project collective, ownership was not strong because of historical conflicts among the participants.	A more consistent idea of leadership developed within a multi nation, science context that incorporated broader stakeholder perspectives. Nevertheless there was still lots of politics involved due to different histories, past experiences with each other, different priorities. One major difference of perspective that arose was whether the purpose was to develop leadership that strengthened the existing field, or whether it should be about expanding the field.	Two key boundary issues needed to be resolved: Should the leadership effort be country focused or regionally focused? Should the core group comprise only of those within the field (i.e., only researchers) or include those who are affected by or able to affect the research activities (e.g., government policy makers, community based actors)?

Table 1.1: Using key systems concepts to explore leadership creation in a science network

Choosing an issue

Now it's your turn.

The primary reason we wrote this book was to help you use systems ideas to address specific issues or situations you are facing. This book is based on systems theories, but it is not a theoretical book. It is a workbook. And it is already time for you to do some work.

You probably know more about systems ideas than you realise. So here's a chance to get your existing knowledge out in the open. The book is structured as a series of exercises. This means you can take an example and use it as the focus of these exercises. Indeed that's probably the best way to use the book. If you don't have a particular example to hand, there are case studies that you can use to guide you through the book.

Choose a particular issue that you are faced with, or situation that you wish to explore systemically. It's important to choose a good example that will help you explore systems issues.

Where to start

Perhaps one of the biggest challenges is knowing where to start a systemic inquiry. Commonly you have to choose one of three options:

Option One: A general situation of interest

Option Two: A particular issue or problem that interests or puzzles you

Option Three: A possible or actual solution to a particular problem that you want to test out.

For instance, there has been a recent spate of burglaries in your neighbourhood. Nothing especially valuable has been stolen but people are feeling less secure. There's a lot of suspicion that the robberies are being carried out by neighbourhood kids, which is creating an air of distrust between neighbours. Let's say that you are interested in this topic.

In Option One your starting question might be: "How can I gain a general understanding of this situation of increasing fear and suspicion?" In Option Two you might start with a problem statement: "Is there a way to help people be less fearful without creating conditions where people will feel even more suspicious of each other?" In Option Three you might start with a question about a possible solution: "How can we establish an effective neighbourhood watch intervention?"

Is any starting option better than the others? We think the answer is yes, Option Two. At this stage of your journey into the systems field you are going to have to trust us on this, but an important thing you will learn from this book is that despite what you may have heard about 'holism', systems thinking is actually more about deciding what to leave out than what to include. Starting at Option One tends to include too much and you are likely to get lost in the enormity of it all. You may go through a whole systemic inquiry and gain no insights that will help you address the situation. Starting at Option Three tends to exclude too much and you risk missing important possible alternative ways to address the situation. So Option Two is a good middle ground.

This is not a hard and fast rule. Sometimes you have no choice but to start at, say, Option Three. Something has happened; someone has come up with a solution and your job is to get the solution to work. As your experience of using systems ideas develops you will be more aware of how to avoid the pitfalls that lurk underneath Options One and Three, but at this stage, for your example to work with in this book, we suggest starting at Option Two. Start with some form of problem statement that doesn't mean you have to consider every conceivable aspect of the situation or doesn't imply a particular solution. Be warned though that many problem statements are solution statements in disguise.

Here are some more tips for choosing a good example:

TEAMWORK

- Ideally the example has to be *important* to you and, if possible, to other interested people, so you can work on it as a team. We've provided an example if you don't have anything, but we strongly recommend you select one from your own experience.
- It is best to choose an example that requires something being done, a *useful intervention* of some kind. Systemic approaches are no more useful in addressing the big unsolvable questions of the universe than anything else.
- The situation has to be puzzling, a *challenge*, wicked. Why bother to use systems ideas when it's obvious what the answer is? Puzzling, challenging and wicked situations also provide the greatest challenge to designing an intervention.
- Remember you are learning new stuff, so choose something where the *potential for learning* is greatest. A really tough situation will require very skilled and experienced use of systems ideas. Mark those down for later when you've a bit more mileage under your belt.

Describing the main features

OK, now back to the task in hand. Take out a piece of paper and write your example down on that paper. Just the main features, and especially what it is that interests or puzzles you about the situation you have described. Don't try to analyse it too much or place too much detail. Just what it is and why you are interested in this situation or puzzle will do for now. As we wrote earlier, focus, if possible, on Option Two type statements. Place this description above the three sheets of large paper.

Materials	Tips / instructions
Three large pieces of paper (flip-chart sheets are ideal)	Lay the sheets on the floor for you to walk around as you think.
Marker pen	Write 'inter-relationships', 'perspectives' and 'boundaries' on the sheets.
Small pieces of paper, e.g., medium sized Post-It notes	Don't be tempted to work any of this case in your mind or on your computer. Trust us, it won't work as well.

Table 1.2: Materials needed for Level One

Description of main features

Table 1.3   Main features of your case

Identify inter-relationships, perspectives and boundaries

Next, write down on the smaller pieces of paper anything about the situation or puzzle that is in some way related to 'inter-relationships' and place it on the relevant large piece of paper. Repeat this for 'perspectives' and 'boundaries'. Don't worry too much about things being 'right'. Don't worry if you are moving back and forth between categories. If you find that some aspects fit in more than one category (e.g., inter-relationships and boundaries), then write one for each category. Don't worry (yet) about precise meanings of inter-relationships, perspectives and boundaries.

TEAMWORK

Once you've finished, take out a further sheet of paper and write down any insights or observations you have about what is now in front of you. Place that below the three sheets of paper. You may also use the template of table 1.4 below.

Inter-relationships	Perspectives	Boundaries
How do things connect with each other? What is the nature of those connections (good, conflicted, close, rapid, weak ...)	*What are the different ways a situation can be understood? How many sentences starting with "Something to do with ..." can you complete?*	*What's in and what's out? With what consequences for whom or what?*
Insights and possible solutions	Insights and possible solutions	Insights and possible solutions

Table 1.4 Template for identifying inter-relationships, perspectives and boundaries at level one.

Enough is enough ... or not?

TEAMWORK

You've just completed your first cycle of a systems based inquiry. It might be superficial or you might feel at this stage that you've gained enough insights to address the situation or puzzle. If you've gained sufficient insights then fine: stop. That's what the project officer did in our example. There's no point in over-analysing a situation. Jump ahead to the section of the book headed 'Wicked Solutions'.

If you feel you haven't gained sufficient insights, then read on.

LEVEL TWO

Three core concepts

Inter-relationships, perspectives, boundaries

Still with us? Excellent. Time now to dig a little further into these three concepts and deepen our analysis and understanding. Firstly, where did these concepts come from? A little history helps. All histories are by their nature simplifications and this is no exception[2].

A short history of the systems field

Systems ideas can be traced back many thousands of years, but the modern systems movement traces its lineage to the middle of the twentieth century, starting in the 1930s and accelerated during the Second World War. You can recognise three main phases since then.

From the early days until the late 1960s, the focus of the systems field was very much on *inter-relationships*. This period represented the 'wiring diagram' phase of thinking systemically and is still influential today. Indeed, some of the mapping approaches (e.g., network maps, concept maps) originated during this first phase.

By the early 1970s, many people in the systems field realised that the relative importance of particular inter-relationships often depended on the different perspectives through which people observed a situation. Think briefly of the first exercise — there are probably many perspectives represented. Thus, systemic thinking began to include the implications of applying different *perspectives*, worldviews or framings to the same situation. It also led to a significant change in the *idea* of systems. Prior to this the systems approach was considered a way of describing how reality was ordered and behaved. Systems were 'real', they were obvious to all and universally agreed upon. This concept of systems as 'real' things is powerful today. In fact it is what most people mean when they talk of 'a system', like the 'health system' or the 'filing system'. However, the systems field moved on from this concept and in this phase, systems became understood as concepts — mental models that allowed us to understand and make sense of the messiness and disorder of reality. This approach tends to talk more about observing situations in systemic ways, rather than observing specifically identified systems.

However, by the mid-1980s, some systems thinkers concluded that focusing on perspectives had its problems. Perspectives influence what we consider relevant or irrelevant; they determine what is 'in' our framing of a situation (the way we understand a situation) and what lies 'outside' that framing. Whoever defines the dominant perspective controls the boundary of a systemic inquiry or intervention. Thus, the importance of studying *boundaries* and critiquing boundary decisions (including those who made them) is the third core concept underpinning a systems approach. Let us look at each of these concepts in turn.

We will do this using another example. This time from South America.

Our example: Rice, malaria, water in Peru[3]

Rice is a major part of the Peruvian diet. Production just about matches domestic demand. There are plans to make rice a major export crop, so new production areas are being developed.

The north eastern region of Peru has become the country's primary rice production area. Since the 1970s new dams and irrigation systems have enabled more than 60,000 small farmers and their families to grow rice in this arid climate. In response to this growth the production in more traditional areas has declined. However, water

---

[2] Loosely based on a description by Gerald Midgley (2000) in his book Systemic Intervention

[3] This example is based on a real case but has been altered to emphasise certain systemic aspects and is not entirely factual.

allocation issues are now a major source of tension within and between communities (including the payment of protection money to gangs). Although malaria is endemic to the community, migrant workers from other rice growing parts of Peru have brought the more serious strain of the disease associated with brain damage. However, it develops gradually over a long time period, and in the short term it is like the local form.

The malarial infection rate of those who work in the rice paddy is high and includes people from most families. Traditional control methods using insecticide require substantial doses to have any impact and are increasingly less effective. Bouts of malaria restricts the labour available to work the paddy fields and affects other activities, such as schooling (which is partly supported by companies that sell insecticides).

Tourists tend to stay away from this very beautiful part of Peru partly because of the malarial problem, although economically tourism is a poor alternative to rice production.

After considerable and difficult discussions with local people, the rice producer cooperatives, local authorities and health services an intervention was developed that would dry out the paddy fields intermittently during the crop growing season. The idea was to break the mosquito breeding cycle but the risk is that it may impact crop production (thus, the cooperatives opposed the project). Farmers are paid on the basis of quantity, quality and consistency of supply.

Inter-relationships

Many newcomers to the systems field are familiar with the idea of inter-relationships. How things are connected and with what consequence stems from the earliest thinking about systems. It is also the concept most strongly embedded in the popular imagination. When we talk about the education system or the health system, we imagine a set of objects and processes that are interconnected in some way. The popularity of system dynamics and complex adaptive systems in many parts of the world cements the notion that inter-relationships are an important systems concept.

However, systemic thinking doesn't concern itself with just any inter-relationships. It focuses especially on particular aspects of them:

Dynamics: How the inter-relationships affect the behaviour of a situation over a period of time.

Non-linearity: How the size of the output or effect of inter-relationships appears unrelated to the size of the input to the inter-relationship. This is often but not always caused by feedback. The simplest example of non-linear relationships is exponential growth patterns familiar in ecology and your bank account.

Context sensitivity: How the same inter-relationships in different contexts have different results. Malaria control methods that work well in Thailand may not work in the Philippines.

Complexity: How to understand inter-relationships that are so complicated or complex that you cannot assess them in terms of simple cause and effect.

Five basic questions for addressing inter-relationships systemically:

1. What is the structure of the inter-relationships within the situation (i.e., how are the parts arranged)?
2. What are the processes between parts of that structure?
3. What is the nature of the inter-relationships (e.g., strong, weak, fast, slow, conflicted, collaborative, direct, indirect)?
4. What patterns that emerge from these inter-relationships over time, with what consequences and for whom?
5. What do you consider are the key inter-relationships?

TEAMWORK

These are not definitive questions, but good places from which to consider how you can make your existing practice be more systemic.

Our example

In the example there are many components (e.g., rice, farmers, disease, water, criminal gangs, national priorities, migration, pesticides, food security, local economic well-being), and the way they interact with each other is very complicated and non-linear. Clearly there is a close relationship between water, mosquitos and malaria, with elements that work both fast (infection) and slow (brain damage). The relationship between water allocation and criminal activity is clearly also closely related, and the relationship between the farmers and the public health officials needed to be highly collaborative and cooperative for the initiative to be implemented. You will think of many others that would take pages to outline, and in Level Three we will show you a way to describe them in a more efficient way than writing paragraph after paragraph. But for Level 2 a shortish list will do. It would be tempting at this stage to say that the key relationships were between water, disease and income.

Perspectives

Just looking at interconnections does not make an inquiry or intervention systemic. People will see and interpret those inter-relationships in different ways depending on their perspectives. A local cafe owner might view issues to do with preventing the spread of Listeria bacteria quite differently than someone from the health service, even though they may 'see' the same thing (i.e., customers getting sick). But there is more to it. What a health inspector does when he or she 'sees' a cafe premises will be different from what the cafe owner does when he or she 'sees' the same thing. Our perceptions promote behaviours that affect the way a situation unfolds. Indeed, what we see as unintended or unexpected patterns within a situation often results from our unwillingness to deeply understand or explore other people's perceptions and subsequent behaviours. We use words like 'unintended effects' without considering that somebody somewhere may indeed have intended them. For us to fully comprehend the inter-relationships and dynamics of a situation we must also identify and understand the range of relevant perspectives that people bring to it. To do so, it is helpful to distinguish between three aspects of perspective: stakeholders, stakes and framings.

Stakeholders are groups of people or things that have a common role in a situation or intervention (e.g., teachers, consumers, writers). Thus, we use the term stakeholder role since some stakeholders can fulfil several roles (e.g., farmer, village leader, cooperative member). In contrast, stakes relate to individual values and motivations (e.g., wealth, honour, fairness, past history, purpose, ideas of professionalism). People with different stakeholder roles may share the same stakes, and any one stakeholder role will contain within it several different (perhaps conflicting) stakes. Stakes are the motivations that underpin stakeholder behaviours, the risks and opportunities that the stakeholder role carries; it's the skin that stakeholders have in the game. We will come back to this in much more detail in Level 3 of this book.

Framings ... "Something to do with ..."

Deliberating on the impact of different stakeholders and stakes gives us an opportunity to frame issues. Framing is a bit more than just listing stakeholder views, although that is often a good place to start. Framing is really trying to work out what the situation is — or could be — *about*. Framing helps you identify how people understand a situation and thus how they behave. Framing is the lens through which you (or others) view the situation or an intervention. An easy way to identify a possible framing (although not always the best way) is to take a stake and add the phrase 'something to do with ...' in front of it.

Some possible framings of a Rolling Stones concert:

- a fun evening out
- income generation
- cultural expression
- marketing product
- nostalgia

Let's assume your interest in a rock concert situation is constructing the list of songs that will be played at the concert. Each of the framings ('something to do with's) in the text box suggests different ways of constructing the play list and thus implies different kinds of songs. If you designed or looked at the task only through a 'fun day out' framing (lots of dance oriented music), you might come up with a very different design or assessment than if you used an 'income generation' framing (where the play list might be more oriented towards promoting the latest iTunes release), or a nostalgia framing (a greatest hits playlist).

Breaking down the situation into different framings would allow you to construct a set list that satisfies most attendees. The population of ageing 70s and 80s rock stars is very skilled at working within multiple framings of their performances, tipping a nod at each of them.

Framings are not necessarily 'right' or 'wrong'. Sometimes seeing things through a different framing helps solve a tricky problem. There's a story[4] told about Russ Ackoff — a key historical figure in the systems field. A big machine tool manufacturer experienced considerable fluctuations in demand for its products. This created problems of low morale, poor productivity and bad industrial relations. Russ was called in to sort out this issue which was framed as a 'production smoothing' problem.

After a considerable amount of thinking around the issue and some failed attempts to model various production scenarios, he encouraged the company to reframe the situation as a 'demand smoothing' issue rather than a 'production smoothing' issue. To smooth demand you needed to find a product that was counter-cyclical to the demand for the company's existing product line. Road-building equipment was found to be counter-cyclical to that for machine tools, but also required much of the same technology and marketing and distribution skills. Fluctuation in demand was reduced to a minimum, which in turn resulted in stable employment. We will explore the issues of stakeholder, stakes and framings in greater detail in Level 3 of this book.

Meantime, here are four useful 'perspective' oriented questions.

TEAMWORK

Four basic questions for exploring perspectives systemically:

6.   Who or what are the key stakeholder roles within the situation?
7.   What are the key stakes?
8.   What are the different ways in which you can understand or frame the situation? Which are the key framings?
9.   How are these different framings going to affect the way in which stakeholders act or expect, and thus need to be considered?

Our example

Clearly, there are many stakeholder roles in this example. But key ones? For the sake of this exercise we identified farmers, migrant paddy field workers, public health workers, pesticide companies, protection gangs and village leaders. Their stakes include health, profit, rice production, power/authority, knowledge, conflict management.

Different framings could be:

- something to do with rice production
- something to do with income generation
- something to do with fair allocation of water
- something to do with health
- something to do with roles in village
- something to do with developing an export industry for rice
- something to do with controlling gang behaviour

---

4 Recounted in Jackson (2002) Systems approaches to management, p. 235.

Clearly the 'formal' framing was 'health', but as we shall see in the next section we cannot understand what happened with this intervention if we only look at it from a 'health' framing. Indeed, we would be greatly misled. So for the sake of this example (and because in truth we know the points we want to make), we will pick three key framings: health, income generation and rice production. Our assumption is that these three framings will engender sufficient support for the whole project, and overcome concerns farmers had about the effect on the growth of rice, provide a way of designing the intervention and, in this case, interpreting the results.

Boundaries

Setting boundaries is not optional. Every endeavour has to set boundaries. You cannot do everything, consider everything, see everything, indeed, monitor everything. A boundary differentiates between what is 'in' and what is 'out', what is deemed relevant and what is irrelevant, what is important and what is unimportant, what is worthwhile and what is not, what suits the one in a position of power and what doesn't, who benefits and who is disadvantaged. Boundaries are the places where values are exposed and disagreements are highlighted.

Key locations of boundary decisions include purpose of intervention, intended beneficiaries, measurement approaches, resource allocation, decision-making authority, necessary expertise (skills, knowledge, who's an expert) and who or what is marginalised, harmed or made victim by an intervention.

Addressing boundaries systemically means that you set boundaries consciously and consider the implications. Broadly speaking there are three core concerns when setting boundaries: ethics, politics and pragmatics.

From an ethical point of view, you hold certain values and those values reflect your ethical stance on things. If you believe that women have an essential role in preventing dengue fever, then you will want your intervention to ensure that their voices are heard and acknowledged.

From a political point of view, you wish your endeavour to be seen as legitimate. Thus, how you set the boundary — and who you include and exclude from that process — will affect that legitimacy.

From a pragmatic point of view, those who are marginalised (or those who represent marginalised interests) are not likely to take things lying down. Some people may not like a strategy to consider the interests of loan sharks in your attempt to address housing foreclosures, but if you don't there's a risk they will oppose your intervention and hinder its execution. You need to work out a way of managing that possibility. So there is a practical reason to explore who or what is marginalised or harmed and see how (or indeed whether) those interests can be accommodated in your intervention.

Your boundary deliberations may change the nature of the intervention. Hence, the iterative nature of boundary questions; they raise the possibility that you may need to reassess your initial judgments on inter-relationships, perspectives and boundaries.

TEAMWORK

Three basic questions for surfacing boundary decisions systemically:

10.   Which key inter-relationships are privileged and which are marginalised? With what effect on whom?
11.   What key perspectives (i.e., stakeholder roles, stakes, framings) are privileged and which are margin-alised? With what effect on whom?
12.   How can you manage the ethical, political and practical consequences of these decisions, especially those that cause harm or have the potential to cause harm because they exclude an inter-relationship or perspective?

Our example

So the key inter-relationships that were privileged were water, disease and income, with quite closely related key stakeholder roles as farmers, paddy field workers, public health workers, pesticide companies, protection gangs and village leaders. Key stakes were health, profit, rice production, power/authority, knowledge, conflict management. The key framings were health, income generation and rice production. Overall, this marginalises leadership roles in the villages, some of the criminal activities, social issues to do with migration and the broader national context. All of which could derail the project for ethical reasons (e.g., what about the local villagers), political reasons (e.g., ignoring the power of the local rice cooperatives) and pragmatic reasons (e.g., insecticide companies removing support from the local schools), which together threaten the sustainability or the ability to spread the initiative. Of course this is unfair on you because we know what actually happened but this list allows us to make some important points. Firstly, and perhaps the main point, is that the health framing was largely irrelevant to the 'success' of the project. Malaria is endemic to the community, is not the major health issue and this new strain takes years to have effect. From the local community point of view, the 'health' perspective — the formal rationale of the project — was imposed by outsiders and irrelevant to them. What made the project succeed — why they collaborated — was that the net income of farmers increased (i.e., income generation). Although the quantity of rice grown declined, the quality increased (i.e., the rice production framing), since the farmers were paid on the basis of both quality as well as quantity. Plus they no longer had the cost of pesticides. This allowed the villagers as a whole to benefit and alleviated the reliance on pesticide companies for educational support. This still left the issue of how to include the interests of the cooperatives, whose authority had been undermined by their initial opposition and how to handle the protection racketeering — but at least the financial success created some negotiation opportunities.

However, returning to our main point, none of this would have been obvious or even feasible if the focus of the entire endeavour had been on the original framing — the reduction of malaria.

Summarising

Systems approaches can be understood as addressing three important factors within a situation: (1) the inter-relationships between aspects of a situation, (2) the perspectives through which that situation can be understood, and (3) the boundaries decisions that are necessary to allow us to address a situation. You can systemically gauge the pertinence of these factors by asking the *twelve basic questions* listed above. Do so for your own case by using the tips in the text box below.

TEAMWORK

Task: Deepening your insight

- Look again at your pieces of paper.
- Go through each of the 12 questions, write your responses, one on each piece of paper, and add to the respective large sheet of paper.
- Look at the piece of paper underneath the three large sheets, the paper that described your ideas from the first pass earlier in this book.
    - o   What insights would you keep?
    - o   What insights would you change?
    - o   What insights would you add?
    - o   What insights would you remove?
- What do those insights imply about resolving your wicked problem and generating an appropriate solution?

Happy to stop here? Or need to go to the next level, the deep dive? If so read on

LEVEL THREE

The deep dive

A method of detailed systemic inquiry

So far in this book, we've given you two rounds of practice in systemic inquiry. The first round, Level One, was based around the three concepts of inter-relationships, perspectives and boundaries. The second round, Level Two, comprised a set of 12 questions based on these three concepts. Hopefully the two rounds came up with some material useful to you. You are about to enter the main section of this book, where we describe a more detailed method of systemic inquiry that digs much deeper into a situation.

The method comprises three stages: one each for inter-relationships, perspectives and boundaries, although each stage comprises a number of steps.

A few points before you put your foot on the first step.

Prepare yourself to take some time on this section of the book, it's not something that can easily be rushed through in an hour or so. Between some steps you might want to go for a walk or have a good sleep. Each stage will require you to work on your own case. If possible, include some other people in your deliberations — there are times when we ask for different perspectives to be considered and that is not always easy when working on your own. To help you work on your own case, we have supplied a detailed case of our own. Take time to understand what we do with that case at each step; you will probably need to refer back to it while working on your own case.

We recommend that you follow every stage of this method — at least the first time you use this method. That's because each stage builds on the previous one. However, you may find you have to move to and fro between the various stages, since later stages may cause you to rethink earlier ones. Over time, with repeated use, you will find your own way through.

The way we proceed through this method is that we focus first on analysing the wicked situation you are interested in, and then move towards designing possible solutions. In real life, of course, things are not as sequential as that. You will be flipping between analysing, designing and implementing in all sorts of orders and in different degrees of depth. You will be redesigning as you implement and your implementation will throw up new analysis. In those circumstances you can modify our method or use the principles that underpin it. Think of it rather like the first time you follow a recipe; subsequent times you will add bits here and there that are based on your own knowledge and preferences ... a bit more garlic here, maybe add some parsley, fry the onions *before* putting the pasta on to boil, and the traditional recipe advice — add salt and pepper to taste.

An overview of Level Three

Issue selection: Typifying the nature of the systemic inquiry

Rich picture drawing: Sweeping in all that may be relevant

Stakeholder analysis: Determining who are most concerned ...

Stake identification ... and what their main concerns are

Formulation of framings: for "seeing through the eyes of another"

Rich picture exploration: Preparatory summary of key elements

Outline of the ideal situation: Objectives are motivated by ideals

Boundary critique: Systemic inquiry into the boundary choices that define the why of 'is' and how of 'ought'

Systemic intervention outline: Finalise your intervention design to improve its overall feasibility, making use of the insights gained from the boundary critique

Final check: Redesign when necessary. A systemic approach is always incomplete.

3.1 Inter-relationships: mapping the wicked problem

Only connect the prose and the passion, and both will be exalted...
Live in fragments no longer.

E.M. Forster

Questions

- What is the structure of the inter-relationships within the situation?
- What are the processes between the elements of that structure?
- What is the nature of the inter-relationships?

Rich picturing

Group exploration is critical to resolving wicked problems. It enhances ownership by the stakeholders and enables communication between them, which in turn reinforces ownership even more. It also provides a space for eliciting tacit knowledge, which may prove essential for re-solving the situation. Representing problem complexity graphically is an effective method for ensuring the fullest possible participation. Rich pictures have been widely used for this purpose. They are perhaps best known as the first step of Soft Systems Methodology, developed by Peter Checkland in the late 1980s[5]. They are used in many organisational development and action learning approaches as well as in counselling.

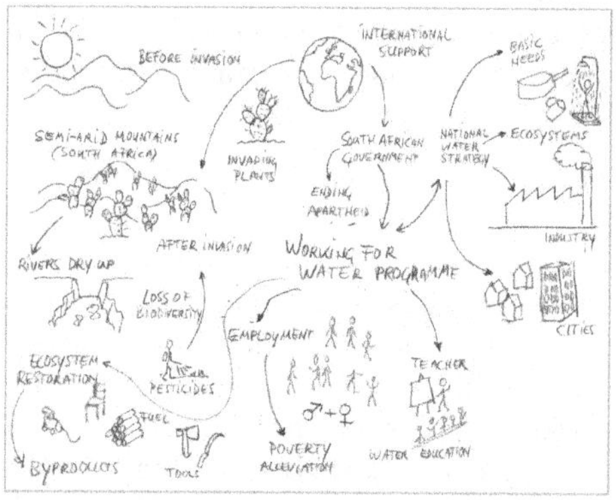

Figure 3.1 Rich picture of the Working for Water Programme in South Africa (adapted from Martin Reynolds, OU, UK)

Rich pictures are well suited for depicting complex situations and their relation with the wider environment. They encapsulate the situation by describing the structures, processes and inter-relationships, but also issues, conflicts, agreements and resources (e.g., people, money, tools, skills). They are hand-drawn and do not require artistic talent. People are often drawn as stick figures, relations as arrows. Labels and text balloons are added to clarify the meaning.

A rich picture can cope with any sort of chaos. It happily receives whatever chaotic mess of thoughts and perceptions pours down your arm from your brain, out of the pen in your hand and onto the page. In the end, a rich picture can be quite messy and confusing in the eyes of a person who was not present during its making. This should not put anybody off from drawing them. Often, the messiest pictures are the richest and most meaningful.

The important thing to understand is that you are *not* drawing a system. In fact you are doing the opposite. You are drawing the unstructured messiness of the situation that will allow you later to think systemically about that situation. Rich pictures are a means for moving from a state of messy confusion, where all you know is that you're dealing with a problematic situation, to a state where you've identified one or more themes that as a group or individual you want to address. These themes are then refined and defined as systems of interest for further exploration (see Steps 2 and 3).

---

5 See the later chapter Further Readings for various references to Checkland's work.

Drawing a rich picture

Ideally, the first thing to do is to recruit a bunch of people with different perspectives on the situation and bring them together in some way. But you may also do it on your own. It just risks being less 'rich'.

Once you've gathered whoever is going to work on this, you will then need a large sheet of paper and some felt tip pens, perhaps also a block of Post-Its.

The big question that worries everyone when starting to draw a rich picture is where to start.

Here's one way. Thinking about the situation or issue, write on separate Post-Its (in all, maybe 20–50):

- Who or what are the key stakeholder roles?
- What are the key stakes (e.g., purposes, motivations, values, norms, aspirations, goals)?

Now place them on the paper in a way that allows you to display the structure of the inter-relationships of stakes and stakeholders within the situation. Once you are happy with the overall configuration, you can remove the Post-Its one by one and start drawing to show:

- the processes between elements of that structure;
- the nature of the inter-relationships (e.g., strong, weak, fast, slow, conflicted, collaborative, direct, indirect);
- important aspects of the situation that affect how the stakeholders, stakes, structures and processes interact. Things like:
- purposes, aspirations, and goals;
- motivations;
- values and norms;
- environmental aspects, e.g., a climate of opinion;
- issues, conflicts, and agreements;
- resources (e.g., people, money, tools, skills);
- things you don't know or puzzle you.

Tip to really free your mind

The benefit of rich pictures is in revealing thoughts you haven't already had, and in saying things you haven't already said. Jake Chapman suggests the following trick to get around this problem. Before asking a group to start drawing, he gets them to write down everything they already think about the situation. The things they always say about it. The things they've already articulated. These thoughts are valuable, but the desire to express them can get in the way of doing the simpler thing: just drawing what you 'see' happening in the situation.

TEAMWORK

Other tips and suggestions [6]

Before you start give your situation a title (e.g., micro-beer distribution in Uganda). For a start it helps draw a boundary around your task, but if you are doing this with others it allows at least an initial conversation. However, **do not phrase it as a problem, a goal or a question** (e.g., how can I get decent beer from Kampala to Entebbe?). Rich pictures are actually trying to stop you rushing too quickly to a problem statement or solution.

It is very important to convey all the important elements of a situation without overly imposing your own understanding and prejudices. Indeed, rich pictures are drawn before you know clearly which parts of a situation you should be focusing on. We often hear about people rushing to solutions. Well, it is equally a problem rushing too quickly to define the problem. Therefore, free your mind as much as possible from any preconceived ideas you may have about the situation. Too many try to place too much order too quickly into a situation. In contrast, a rich picture displays as much of the situation as possible.

---

[6] Drawing extensively from http://systems.open.ac.uk/materials/T552/pages/rich/richAppendix.html

For many the value of rich pictures is only revealed once they start using them with others, perhaps in a group. Looking at what different people in the same group contribute, and then comparing pictures between groups, is an effective way of revealing these differences because they express things you wouldn't think of saying. And sometimes they allow you to say in a simple and unthreatening way things that may have seemed rude or frivolous to articulate. They can also help you to see things you might otherwise have missed: connections, traps, possibilities, contradictions, and so on.

If you are working in a group, there's one important rule. Use only one drawing implement! Otherwise you get half a dozen small unconnected rich pictures being drawn, and it also forces conversation. Generally speaking just encourage people to start — you will be surprised how quickly people get into the spirit. However, a New Zealand colleague of ours, Judy Oakden, makes the perceptive comment that rich picture drawing works best when the group has 'formed'. In other words, it isn't a good warm-up exercise. The group needs to work out its dynamic, decide what might be confidential, and identify who knows what and whom. It is even a good idea to show some examples of rich pictures and go through the Open University rich picture building exercise described at the end of this chapter. She finds it best to have people just talk in a guided or facilitated way for a while rather than filling out cards and pinning them on the wall. If this is well facilitated it helps the group move more quickly into the areas they don't understand or puzzle them. It also helps establish the group dynamic.

People will possibly feel uncomfortable and uncertain during the process. It can be hard to face other people's often surprisingly different assumptions, because this make us question our own assumptions. This can be demanding and unsettling. It can mean throwing away the solutions we thought we had, going back to the beginning and starting afresh. But that's often exactly what is needed at the start of a systemic inquiry. So reassure them that these feelings are normal during the process, but it will be worth their while

People may feel overwhelmed when they have finished the picture, again reassure them this is normal. Part of this sense is because they think that taking a systems approach means they have to take everything in the rich picture into account. This is where you can remind them that the systems approach is about being very smart about what to leave out rather than what to put in.

Do's and don'ts

It is essential that every line drawn between two elements has an explanation attached to it. Otherwise you have no idea what the line actually means, or how powerful it is, how much agreement there is, what is carried by the inter-relationship. Also avoid double headed arrows, since inter-relationships are rarely equal. Draw and describe two lines instead.

Don't have the piece of paper too big. Two sheets of flip chart paper taped together is usually enough.

Make sure that your picture includes not only the factual data about the situation, but also the subjective information. You need to show all that you perceive as problematic or significant emotions and relationships as well as groupings and connections of various sorts.

Look at the social roles that are regarded within the situation as meaningful by those involved, and look at the kinds of behaviour expected from people in those roles. If you see any conflicts, indicate them.

Do not seek to impose any style or structure on your picture. Place the elements on your sheet wherever your instinct prompts. At a later stage you may find that the placement itself has a message for you.

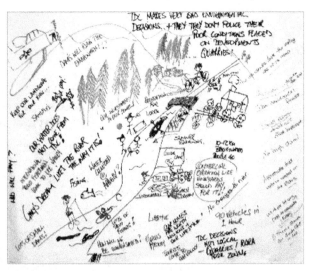

Figure 3.2   Rich pictures can be quite messy

Do not think in systems terms as in, "Well, the situation is made up of a marketing system and a production system and a quality control system." There are two reasons for this. The first is that the word 'system' implies organised interconnections and it may be precisely the absence of such organised interconnectedness that lies at the heart of the matter; therefore, by assuming its existence (by the use of the word system) you may be missing the point. Note, however, that this does not mean that there won't be some sort of link or connection between your graphics, as mentioned above. The second reason is that doing so will channel you down a particular line of thought, namely the search for ways of making these systems more efficient.

If you are working as a group be aware of any politics and power dynamics.

Finally, don't be put off by the idea of drawing a picture. Most books that use rich picturing display nice, neat, well-honed pictures that create the idea that you need to be an artist to do it properly. In contrast figure 3.2 is a rich picture that is wonderfully messy and inartistic yet still useful. It describes a water-use issue in New Zealand.[7]

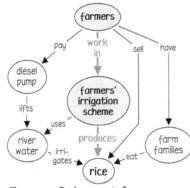

Figure 3.3   Basic concept of
an irrigation scheme

Figure 3.4   Diesel pump irrigating rice along a Sahelian river

Our case example: lift irrigation along Sahelian rivers

Given that we are asking you to work through this book using your own example, it seemed only fair that we should work in parallel with you on an example of our own.

The example concerns lift (i.e. pump assisted) irrigation in sub-Saharan Africa. Immediately south of the Sahara desert lies a geographical area known as the Sahel. It stretches from the Atlantic coast of Senegal eastward for thousands of kilometres all across West and Central Africa. It has annual rainfall figures in the range of 200–600 mm/year, which is barely enough for agriculture, yet many people live there. Some of these people are pastoralists, like the Peul (also known as Hausa) or Tuareg. Others, such as the Songhai, are sedentary farmers who used to grow deep-water rice or dry-season sorghum in the floodplains of the great rivers that traverse the area. The best known of these rivers is the Senegal River, forming the frontier between Senegal and Mauritania, and the Niger River that flows all the way from Guinea to Nigeria, traversing Mali and Niger on its 4000 km path to the ocean. In the early 1970s and 1980s, the Sahel suffered a number of devastating droughts and subsequent low rainfall from which traditional agriculture never recovered. Since the first great droughts, development and

---

7 Ann Winstanley, Virginia Baker, Jeff Foote, Jan Gregor, Wendy Gregory, Maria Hepi, Gerald Midgley (2005) Water in the Waimea Basin: Community Values and Water Management Options. A Report by ESR for the Waimea Water Augmentation Committee and the Tasman District Council.

government agencies have worked to introduce diesel-powered lift irrigation for the production of green-revolution rice as an alternative to the defunct traditional crops. Irrigation schemes ranged in size from 3 to 100 ha, depending on the size and number of pumps. Most of the pumping equipment was procured from European OECD countries. It proved difficult to introduce lift irrigation in a sustainable manner: most farmer groups failed to renew pumps after withdrawal of the successive aid programmes.

We will analyse the case to show how the systems approach of this book works and what could be its utility, but we do not claim to be able to have found the magic solution. After all, the sustainability of pump irrigation in the Sahel has all the hallmarks of a wicked problem. Moreover, any (re-)solution of a wicked problem is only as good as the people participating. And we are the only ones participating in this exercise; in real life we'd be involving as many key stakeholders as possible. After all, it is their wicked problem as much as ours (although of course they may 'see' it in quite different ways).

What is the problem situation?

What is our (and maybe others') sense of unease with this situation? What's the mismatch between what is, what might, could or ought to be?

For us, there is a concern that the current form of village irrigation development is probably unsustainable. Everybody wants it to be less dependent on external donors, but clearly current efforts are leading to greater, not lesser dependency. If you recall the three options for choosing the case study, our situation of interest reflects Option Two: a statement of a particular problem. There is no current implied solution (i.e., Option Three) and it isn't a broad statement about village irrigation (i.e., Option One). We are concerned about the failure of making pump-based lift irrigation sustainable. That is our problem situation.

Formulating a good strategy is crucial to project effectiveness, even when introducing something as mundane as a pump. Many a simple idea — take the smart phone — has huge implications. There were big winners and big losers, entirely new ways of engaging with the world. So now take a look at the rich picture of the situation that the pump proposal is entering — and just how powerful such a simple device could be in affecting that situation in good and bad ways. It really challenges the ideas that there are unintended events — someone, somewhere in the situation probably intended it. It's only you that didn't. In systems approaches there are no side effects, just effects.

As you look at our rich picture on the following page, think how concise it is. How many pages would it have taken to describe this situation in words alone? Would you have bothered to read them? Would you have remembered them? Would you have been able to link different aspects of the situation? That's the power of rich picturing.

A more detailed description of our rich picture in figure 3.5 will be provided later under the heading 'Re-exploring the rich picture'.

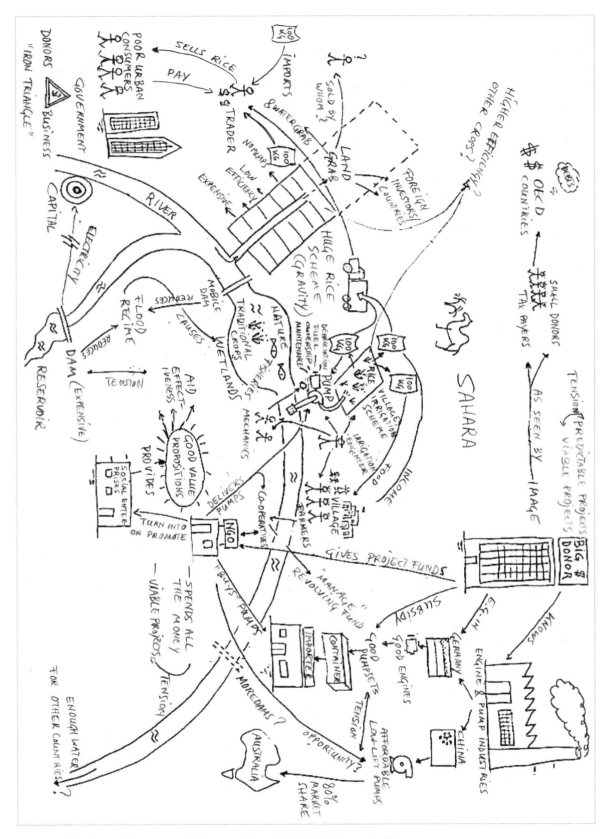

Figure 3.5 Rich picture of the case example: how to make smallholder irrigation sustainable.

Your task

TEAMWORK

Your job now is to take your situation and draw, ideally with others, a rich picture. Take some time out to do it. Don't be tempted to skip this stage and think you already know the key aspects of the situation. That very assumption should be a warning sign that maybe you need to think a little more systemically.

Take as much time as you need, but no longer. Some of the best rich pictures can be done quickly, sometimes they need a bit of care and thought. We'll let you be the judge; you will know when enough is enough. And you can always add to it as you gain insights as you dive further into the process. Once you've finished jot down any insights you have. Can you add them to the rich picture?

If you are still unsure about what a rich picture is and how to construct one, check out the following Open University website: http://systems.open.ac.uk/materials/T552/pages/rich/rp-miners.html

It describes how the rich picture in figure 3.6 was constructed step by step.

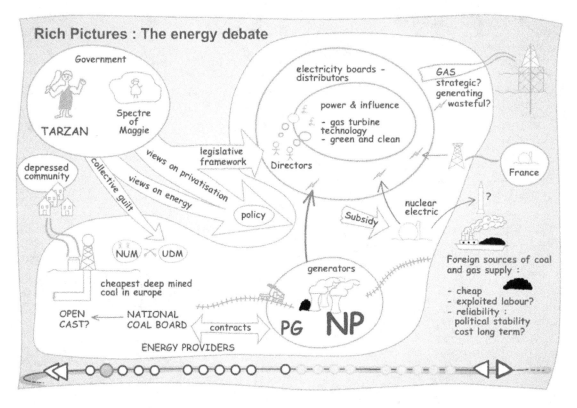

Figure 3.6 One more example of a rich picture

Summary of section 3.1 Inter-relationships

Rich pictures are well suited for depicting complex situations and their relation with the wider environment. They encapsulate the situation by describing the structures, processes and inter-relationships, but also issues, conflicts, agreements and resources. With 'inter-relationships' we mean the configuration of elements, processes and context that make up or characterise the wicked problem or problematic situation.

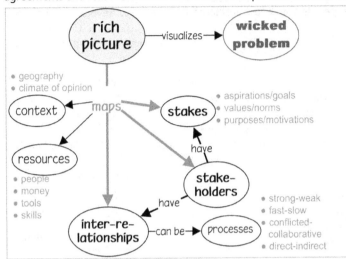

Figure 3.7   Concept map of rich picture drawing

Drawing a rich picture takes place in two stages: (1) arrange 20–50 Post-Its of key stakeholders and key stakes on a large sheet of paper, (2) draw the key stakeholders and key stakes as well as any other elements and processes you consider relevant.

Avoid imposing your own understanding and prejudices. Make sure to bring out not only factual data but also subjective information. Pay special attention to the stakes, such as the goals, values, and motivations of stakeholders.

3.2 Perspectives: framing for purpose

'When I use a word,' Humpty Dumpty said in rather a scornful tone, 'it means just what I choose it to mean — neither more nor less.'

'Through the Looking Glass' : Lewis Carroll

Questions

- What are the different ways in which you can understand or frame the situation?
- What are key framings for gaining adequate insight in the situation?

Perspectives and framings

In the section that briefly describes the development of systems ideas, we mentioned that the introduction of perspectives revolutionised systems approaches. It implied that systems weren't 'real' in the sense that they were self-evident objects. There is no such 'thing' as the filing system, or the banking system, or the school system. If half a dozen people were asked to draw their local transport system, you'd end up with half a dozen — maybe more — different diagrams. Each of these are systems of understanding, conceptual tools by which each person sought to describe and understand transportation in their area.

Thus, in wicked situations the task is not to identify *the system*, but *to understand how people think systemically about the messy reality* that you observed when you drew your rich picture.

In this section you will draw different perspectives out of your rich picture. You will do so in a structured way, by using stakeholder and stake analyses. We call these particular perspectives framings. We are drawing our inspiration here from another stage of Checkland's Soft Systems Methodology, although the match isn't perfect[8]. Framings are simple ways of describing how different people may understand — or frame — their activities or role in a real world situation. It's the way they make sense of a situation, an idea, an intervention or an experience. Consciously or unconsciously, framings guide people's take on problematic situations. Several simultaneous framings can be at work in a person's understanding. Have a look at the framings of a school system in the text box. All these are perfectly plausible and valid framings, even though some of them may not be discussable let alone admitted.

Identifying different framings is important because they provide a key to unlock understanding how people act in situations. If a riot broke out in your local school, you are not going to get many insights if you frame the school system in terms of exam production or childcare. But you might if you frame the school system in terms of community identity. It might suggest exploring things like family rivalries or income disparities. Also as we mentioned in the introduction, people active in the situation will reflect a range of framings and will respond according to those framings.

So if you wish to understand how a situation operates in real life; if you want to know how to design an appropriate intervention   — the purpose of this book — you have to understand the important framings that influence people's behaviours. Only after having identified the framings you can see how different people balance different sets of framings for the best possible outcome. And only after different people have learned how others balance their framings, it will be possible to collaborate towards a resolution that accommodates the different points of view.

> **Some possible ways of seeing and framing a school system**
> - Preparing young people for examinations.
> - Learning things you need in adult life.
> - Disseminating values, norms, customs and habits.
> - An expression of community identity.

Step 1: Conducting a stakeholder analysis

You can guess framings but the risk is that you end up reflecting just your own ways of framing a situation. It is more reliable to do it in a more systemic way, in particular through a deep investigation of stakeholders and stakes. This exploration has two stages:

- Identification of stakeholders and stakeholder roles
- Identification of stakes

Although we describe these as two separate stages, we suggest you think of the process as iterative, moving backwards and forwards through the stages.

How to identify stakeholders

We briefly covered the concepts of stakeholders and stakes in the rich picture process. In the next tasks we are going to explore the issue of stakeholders (or, as we pointed out earlier, more precisely, stakeholder roles, since any one person can undertake several stakeholder roles) and

> **Stakeholders:** those able to affect or be affected by a situation.
>
> **Stakeholder roles:** the roles enacted by individual stakeholders. Individual stakeholders can act out several roles

stakes in greater depth. While doing so, you might want to revisit your rich picture efforts again. This only emphasises how iterative systemic inquiry is. Although we describe our inquiry in this book as a progressive process, it is always wise to go back to earlier stages and see if your new insights change your old ones.

---

8 Checkland (2000) calls them holons: plausible purposeful perspectives that give meaning to real world activities.

Stakeholders are usually individual people, groups of people, organisations or institutions who can affect or be affected by a situation, but that isn't always the case. For instance, if you are an environmentalist or animal rights activist then you'd regard plants and animals as stakeholders. The problem is that in any given situation there may be dozens of possible stakeholder roles and categories. A laundry list of stakeholder roles isn't going to help you towards framing. You need to squash the list down to those that are likely to be key stakeholder roles.

Stakeholder analysis is a good way of shortening the list and a quick web search will bring up many different methods. Here's a simple approach that will get you started. Table 3.1 shows our stakeholder analysis based on the stated problem situation: that the current form of village irrigation development is unsustainable. Note how some of these roles could be undertaken by one person (e.g., village leader, farmer, rice consumer, irrigation expert).

Table 3.1   Stakeholder analysis for the irrigation project in terms of the problem situation

Stakeholder roles	... have an impact on	... are impacted by	Importance
Big overseas donors (e.g., USAID, Gates Foundation)	• the choice and design of irrigation projects • selection of pumps	• tax payers • overseas governments • Bill and Melinda Gates	++
NGOs	• selection of pumps	• donor money flow • consensus about project design logic	+
Irrigation expert	• field implementation of village irrigation scheme	• short-term practicalities	+
Farmers	• financial sustainability of village irrigation scheme	• poverty, hunger • predictability of river flow • consensus about project design logic	++
Village leaders	• irrigation scheme management	• farmers' willingness-to-pay for irrigation	++
National or local government	• project permission/design • river basin management, river flow (timing, qty.) • food & agricultural policy	• local interest groups • voters • donors (priorities, $$)	+
Pump importers & dealers	• the type of pumping equipment available	• project design • donor preferences • manufacturer	++
Rice consumers	• rice imports	• price of rice, low income	+

Your task

Look back at your rich picture and think of the situation. Then complete table 3.1, if possible with other people.

Add as many rows as you like.

TEAMWORK

- 'Impact on' relates to the influence or control the stakeholder role has on the situation you are interested in, or the intervention you are planning. It is important to identify whether it helps or hinders either or both.
- 'Impacted by' relates to the impact felt by this stakeholder role, which could be positive or negative.

- 'Importance' relates to broader factors about the stakeholder role. For instance, in terms of the school riot example, the janitors may or may not have much impact on or are impacted by the school riot, but they have a deep understanding of how the school operates below the radar.

It's probably best to do this in a couple of cycles. On the first cycle you might just want to record high, medium, low in terms of scale of impact, and positive (+), negative (-), neutral or both in terms of nature of impact. In subsequent iterations, or once you have narrowed the list to less than half a dozen, you might want to add a more detailed description.

In general terms you'll want to highlight those in the list that record high on all three counts. It is also wise to have about a third of the list associated with negative impacts or being negatively impacted. Try to keep these key stakeholder roles to less than six.

Name of stakeholder role	Impact of stakeholder role on situation or your intervention	How stakeholder role is impacted by situation or your intervention	Importance to situation or your intervention

Table 3.2: Template for identifying key stakeholders

Step 2: How to identify stakes

Stakes are the hidden time bomb in a situation. They provide the key to understanding the behaviour of situations and the success of interventions, often far more than just identifying stakeholders and stakeholder roles. Stakes are what drive stakeholders to do what they do, they are an amalgam of motivations, values, beliefs, roles, cultural norms and aspirations. The importance of stakes is easy to overlook. It is even easier for them to become oversimplified stereotypes (e.g., politicians driven by greed, activists driven by anger).

Stakes: the values and motivations that stakeholders bring to a situation when enacting their stakeholder roles (e.g., wealth, honour, fairness, past history, purpose, ideas of professionalism).

Importantly, people reflecting different stakeholder roles may share the same stakes, and any one stakeholder role will contain within it several different and perhaps conflicting stakes. Indeed, how people juggle their own conflicting stakes (and perhaps stakeholder roles) goes a long way to understanding behaviour in certain situations. It's certainly critical to issues of sustainability.

Stakeholder roles	Stakes	Importance
Big overseas donors (e.g., USA, Gates Foundation)	Sustainable projects	++
	Reducing hunger	+
NGOs	Continuous flow of projects	+
	NGO mission	+

Irrigation expert	Efficient implementation	+
	Access to pumps	+
Farmers	Growing enough food for family	++
	Access to pumps	++
	Farm income	++
	Sustainable projects	++
Village leaders	Best possible deal for the village	+
	Leadership	+
National or Local Government	National food production	+
Private sector importers & service providers	Profit, turnover, market share	+
	Sustainable projects	+
Rice consumers	Low food prices	++

Table 3.3: Stakeholder roles and stakes

The best starting point is with the key stakeholder roles you've already identified. Ask yourself: What are the key stakes distributed among the stakeholder roles? When addressing this question, you will see why we suggested including stakeholders who negatively affect or are negatively affected by the situation or your intervention.

Contrasting the negative and positive are very good ways of identifying key stakes, including, not unimportantly, your own stakes in this process!

Your task

Start simple by completing a grid like table 3.4. You can make it more complicated in later iterations. Rank the stakes by their importance to the stakeholder, so as to avoid the laundry list. Narrow the list down to about four to six key stakes.

TEAMWORK

Stakeholder roles	Stakes	Importance

Table 3.4: Template for stake identification

Step 3: Selecting key framings

So, finally, we get to framings. By now important ways of framing the situation (and thus the focus of your intervention) should be suggesting themselves.

A framing is a form of perspective that allows you to consider or address a situation in a particular way. It gives meaning to and helps make sense of your intervention. It is a way of seeing or a way of understanding rather than an opinion or result. It's often very different from the formal purpose of an intervention. We suggested a few framings about rock concerts earlier. As another example, one of us once gained great insights by framing an intervention formally supposed to improve technical management skills (Framing #1 = skill development) by adding two other framings into the mix: validation of existing skills (Framing #2 = skill recognition) and networking opportunities for senior and middle managers (Framing #3 = networking).

It's easy to overcomplicate this step. The easiest way to start the framing process is to place the phrase "something to do with" in front of a key stake. So in our example the some key stakes could be:

Something to do with *sustainable projects*

Something to do with *village leadership*

Something to do with *access to pumps*

While on their own these framings provide valuable insights, it's even better when you explore the consequences of different framings. But how do you pick the ones that will give you the best combined set of insights?

Tips for selecting a set of framings

We often get asked to explain the logic of how you get from stakeholder roles and stakes to framings. We've given you one way ('something to do with [stake]), but in truth it isn't an entirely logical task — compared with identifying stakeholders and stakes, selecting a set of framings that are critical to your intervention is more intuitive than analytical. However, the following questions helped us develop useful sets of framings:

- Are the framings properly phrased? A framing is a 'way of seeing' or a 'way of understanding' (e.g., something to do with school as peaceful community) rather than an opinion (e.g., bad kids should be punished) or result (e.g., fewer fights between students).
- Are the framings distinctively different? Even better, are they slightly in tension with each other?
- Are the framings important? Do you expect that individually and collectively they will lead to substantial insights?
- As a rule of thumb, three well-chosen framings are usually sufficient to gain adequate insights into a situation or an intervention. You tend to find that more framings not only generate a lot more work, but often don't lead to many more insights.

If you get completely stuck staring at a blank sheet of paper or screen, then consider the formal purpose of the intervention and ask yourself what kind of world view or focus the formal purpose implies. For instance, if the formal purpose is to address the problem of drowning in rivers, then clearly 'swimming skills' is a potential framing. But is that all there is? If you just focused on swimming skills would it actually reduce drownings? Maybe 'rescue' is another framing that would suggest an additional range of strategies that may make the overall intervention more powerful. Or even a 'water control' framing might be appropriate if the river has sluices and dams further upstream that control the flow.

In our example, we decided, after an awful lot of discussion about the pros and cons of different options, several iterations of 'something to do with ...' that the following three framings would help us gain the best and most diverse insights for addressing our wicked problem.

If these framings are indeed important, they can be expected to lead to new collective insights that will be reflected in the final intervention design.

Framings		
Food production	Income generation	Market for pumps

Table 3.5: Framings for the irrigation project

Your task

Your task is to formulate a few framings for your own case:

Framings		
………………………	………………………	………………………

Table 3.6: Template for framing your own case

TEAMWORK

Framing the quick way

As you have noticed, this section of the book is much more structured than the one on rich picturing. Perhaps you want to know all the steps globally before getting into the nitty-gritty of following all these rules and filling out all those tables, or you simply find it expedient to do so, or you feel highly confident that you can guess the key framings straight away. For just such an occasion, we have prepared a shortlist of stages you may still want to go through quickly before doing so. Here it is.

Looking at your rich picture:
- List those stakeholder roles that have the largest impact on the situation. The impact can be positive or negative.
- List the stakes that are the most powerful influences in the situation. The influence could be positive or negative.
- Compare the list of stakeholder roles and stakes and consider their impact on the situation. What issues arise out of these impacts?
- Looking at issues, what are the different ways of understanding what the situation is about or how people understand what it is all about. Complete the phrase 'something to do with …'
- Now decide which of these framings are going to give you the best insights that will inform your work. These will be your key framings.

Summary of section 3.2 Perspectives

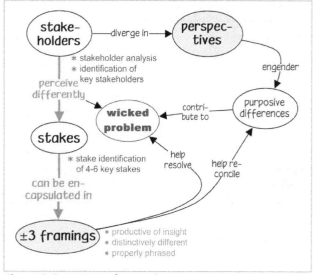

Figure 3.8: Concept map of perspectives

To a large extent, wicked problems are caused by differences between the roles stakeholders possess and the skin they have in the game (which we call 'stakes'). For effective intervention design, these differences must be exposed and hopefully reconciled. This section explains how to find common purposes in the divergent perspectives of the key stakeholders. This is done in three steps: (1) identifying the key stakeholders using stakeholder analysis, (2) identifying and ranking their stakes and (3) from these stakes and stakeholder roles, derive about three framings. Framings comprise the way people make sense of a situation, an idea, an intervention or an experience. Jointly, these framings loosely demarcate the potential ways of intervening in the wicked problem.

3.3 Boundaries: critique for impact

'Tut, tut, child!' said the Duchess. 'Everything's got a moral, if only you can find it.'

'Alice's Adventures in Wonderland': Lewis Carroll

Questions

- How do key framings affect the main boundary issues?
- How can we analyse the motivations and values, power structures and control, expert assumptions and other relevant knowledge, and the ethics of possible interventions?
- How can we handle differences or conflicts among stakeholder views?

You cannot do everything. You cannot see everything. In that sense the idea of 'holism' is an impossibility. Setting boundaries, deciding what is 'in' and what is 'out', what's 'important' and what's 'unimportant' involves tough choices, but every endeavour is bounded. While it is perfectly reasonable to acknowledge different perspectives, someone somewhere decides which perspectives prevail. As a systems practitioner you will not only acknowledge that necessary decision, but also accept that you bear some responsibility for the consequences.

You have already chosen some boundaries in your book tasks. What do you think they may be?

When you chose your key framings you drew boundaries. As you think about your intervention based on those framings you will draw more boundaries. In fact, to repeat ourselves one more time, every endeavour draws many boundaries. Since you can't examine every boundary choice critically, which ones do you focus on? Our guides through this process are C. West Churchman[9], and especially Werner Ulrich whose Critical Systems Heuristics provides the basis for this section of the book[10,11]. Like many systems thinkers they argued that every system has to have a *purpose*. Since any one purpose is a choice selected from many possible purposes, those who choose that purpose have an ethical responsibility to assess the impact of that choice on both those who benefit and those who do not benefit from the purpose. Having chosen that purpose there is now an obligation to ensure that the intervention has adequate *resources* that are managed and controlled in a way that stays true to the purpose and that the system has adequate and appropriate *knowledge* to inform the means to achieve its purpose. Finally, an intervention will only be allowed to happen or have the desired impact if it has appropriate degrees of *legitimacy*. This legitimacy depends not only on those who benefit from the purpose (that's the easy part), but also on those who are made victims by it (i.e., are excluded, deliberately or otherwise, from the intervention). So the key boundary choices that need the highest level of critique, concern purpose, resources, knowledge and legitimacy.

A simple boundary exploration: holiday in Nepal

You may be just a little puzzled about the practical relevance of all this. So let's consider the simple case of a teacher who plans to go on holiday to Nepal. Now what boundary issues will this teacher have to consider (consciously or unconsciously) in her decisions about this trip?

Purpose
Firstly how will she know whether the holiday was or was not a success? That will depend on the purpose of her trip. If it was for fitness, then climbing up to 5000 metres will be deemed a good measure of success, but if it was

---

for spiritual enlightenment then altitude may be an irrelevant measure. How she decides what is and what is not a good measure of success will be an important boundary choice. And in any case should she be the only beneficiary? Who else ought to benefit from her trip?

Resources
What resources will she need and not need? What resources should she be in control of and what resources should she allow other people to control? She only has school holidays and a teacher's income, so clearly money and time are two resources she needs to control. But where should the boundary be set over equipment? What equipment should she have control over and thus be held responsible should there be any negative consequences, and what equipment should not be her choice? What choices lie completely out of the control of anyone who is involved with her trip? That will depend on the purpose but also depend on issues to do with her choice of travel agent, guide and available technology.

Knowledge
What knowledge must be available for planning and for judging whether the knowledge or expertise she is using is accurate? Just how reliable are each of the tour guides and the hundreds of websites claiming to know everything about the Annapurna 16 day circuit? How and where does she set the boundary of demonstrated and relevant expertise that will minimise the likelihood of her purpose being unfulfilled?

Legitimacy
Trekking in Nepal is controversial. It is criticised for damaging the environment; recent landslides created by deforestation for fuel have destroyed entire villages and many people have died. There are human rights issues in terms of the conditions that porters are expected to work. How can she decide how much damage to the environment or local cultures is sufficiently acceptable so that her trip has some legitimacy in the eyes of her colleagues back home?

That seemed easy didn't it? Our example was kept deliberately simple; it lacks all the preceding work we did on inter-relationships and perspectives, culminating in the definition of three framings. There is also no description of the problematic situation to be resolved, no specific critique. Consequently, the example lacks a clear focus; it raises a bunch of boundary questions without any obvious way of addressing them. To show you that our approach has real bite, we will take you stage-by-stage through our example. Once you've done that, we will guide you through your own case.

As we wrote earlier, in this book you, and we, have already taken several boundary decisions. In our and your case studies, decisions have been taken about which stakeholder roles are held to be primary, what stakes are deemed more significant, which issues are considered most important to address and what framings will predominate. You and we now have to explore the consequences of these choices in more detail.

A word of warning. You may not find the tasks we are about to set you easy. In fact we would be rather suspicious if you did find them easy. This book is about addressing wicked problems and it if was easy to address them then there would be no need for this book.

Depending on how challenging you find the boundary critique you may be very tempted at times to slide into less critical frames of mind and opt for soft answers. For that reason we suggest you don't do this process on your own; at the very least have someone leaning over your shoulder keeping you focused. Set aside a decent period of time — maybe don't try to do it all in one session. And be prepared to alter and change things as you go along — don't feel you have to aim for a 'right' answer. You'd be amazed how much discussion took place between us while developing and refining the boundary critique of our example. It probably took the same amount of time as the rest of the book put together. And why not? We are, after all, considering the very core of why we are interested in this particular wicked problem.

So let's step off into the world of *boundary critique*. As we stated earlier we are going to use, as our base, a set of heuristics developed by Werner Ulrich called Critical System Heuristics (CSH), aided by further developments by Martin Reynolds with some additional twists of our own. They are heuristics for the systemic inquiry of intervention designs, which help you structure the questions that enable you to find out whether the intervention is viable or not. Before we submit our case study to this task, and before you submit yours to scrutiny, it's useful to step through the ideas that underpin the tasks we are about to do. It will be a bit of a read, so take your time.

The heuristics

Purpose and beneficiaries

At its simplest, any intervention has a purpose (**P**) that is intended to serve particular needs of intended beneficiaries (**B**) or clients or customers. In the case of an industrial firm they may include employees, stockholders, and suppliers. The decision-makers (D) are responsible for certain resources (R) under their control, which they can allocate for specific purposes. From a management point of view, proper control and allocation of the resources are the direct concern of the decision-makers, while the beneficiaries are concerned whether the purpose really serves their needs. If not, the intervention lacks justification.

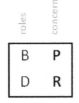

Our first boundary question is how do we know whether the beneficiaries have benefitted? Measures of success (**M**) — in the broadest sense — indicate whether the purpose of serving particular needs for intended beneficiaries is indeed achieved. These are often treated as if they were a technical problem, but as we illustrated in the Nepal trip, the decision over which measures are acknowledged as relevant or valid is based on cultural and professional value judgments that need to be scrutinised.

In practical terms, below are some questions that will help your boundary determination and critique that concern purpose, beneficiaries and measurement. We will be applying them to our case study soon, and then give you the opportunity to apply them to yours.

You will see that we use these questions in two ways: an *Is mode* and an *Ought mode*. Ulrich developed these two modes as a means of helping identify boundaries and assisting the critique, in particular critiquing the 'is' description on the basis of the 'ought' description. Basically you are contrasting the situation as it is right now, with your view (or your and others' views) on what the new design of the system ought to be. The tension between the two brings boundary choices and their consequences to the fore.

> You may be tempted to see the 'is' as 'the problem'. Instead, you should describe the 'is' mode in non-normative terms, reflecting the multiple perspectives and not just your opinion.

'Is' mode questions:

- What transformation or significant change do we observe? This question helps you to look critically at the stated **P**urpose (see also next question).

- What implied **P**urpose best describes this change? Your answer is likely to reflect one of the framings, in one way or the other.

- To what wider agenda (and whose agenda) might this **P**urpose belong? Your answer is likely to provide a rationale for the way the 'is' mode is justified.

- Who or what are the **B**eneficiaries[12] of this purpose?

'Ought' mode questions:

---

12 The term 'beneficiary' can cover persons, groups or other entities. Potential beneficiaries can be found by benefit-cost mapping, which is another way of asking who or what is positively affected by an intervention. Beneficiaries ought to be part of (or internal to) the systems, whereas victims are external. Victims are identified by asking who or what is negatively affected or marginalised by an intervention. By definition, there will always be victims.

- What transformation or significant change do we desire? You may find possible answers by looking at the work you did for the rich picture and the framings.

- What **P**urpose best describes this change? Look at the framings! You may want to describe this in a fairly open way, leaving sufficient options in subsequent planning parameters.

- What wider agenda (and whose agenda) might this **P**urpose belong? This question helps you identify support for 'ought' mode initiatives.

- Who or what ought to be the **B**eneficiaries of this purpose? You may find alternative or additional beneficiaries from those you identified for the same question in the 'is' mode.

Questions for both modes:

- Who benefits from and who is harmed by the system? This question asks you to conduct a benefit-cost mapping, which may help you identify alternative **B**eneficiaries.

- How robust are your arguments that these are the 'right' **B**eneficiaries? Strange as this may sound, it can be surprisingly tempting to pick the 'wrong' beneficiaries.

- Do some of those in influential positions have other **P**urposes (e.g., 'hidden agendas')? How should the implications be handled? Hidden agendas are best identified by 'unfolding' the benefit map.

- How can we know if the beneficiaries benefit; how 'is' and 'ought' this be identified and measured? There will be some **M**easures of success that we can identify and implement, but there will be some that for a variety of reasons cannot be adopted for political or cultural reasons, and thus are chosen to be outside the boundary. Some will always be outside the boundary because we have no way of implementing those measures. You will note that the **M**easures of success or indicators depend on what purpose you chose.

Critique of the 'is' from the position of the 'ought':

- What further comments do you have when comparing the 'is' with the 'ought'?

Resources and decision-makers

We now turn to the issue of control of resources (**R**) by decision-makers (**D**). The core boundary issue is not so much what the decision-makers actually control, but the resources over which they have no control — those that lie in what's called the decision environment (**E**), yet are critical to successful implementation. How so? Some resources will always be outside the decision-makers' control. Some of these will be outside our system — they are givens, there is no boundary choice being made. However, some are *chosen* to be outside their control by actors *within* the system. Why? It's not a good idea to have *all* the necessary resources under the control of the decision-makers in order to maintain checks and balances, to oblige decision-makers to collaborate with others, or be held accountable or responsible for wise and relevant use of the necessary resources. That's why we hold back sweets from our children. The most familiar example is the distinction made between the management of an organisation and its Board of Directors. But who decides which resources lie outside the control of decision-makers (i.e., the resource controllers) is a value-laden boundary choice that requires critique. So too is how to handle the consequences of those resources outside the systems control.

So some questions that will help us:

'Is' mode questions:

- Who makes the key **D**ecisions related to this purpose and the beneficiaries? Who currently does this?

- What **R**esources are available to the decision-makers to ensure that the beneficiaries benefit and the purpose fulfilled?

- What things outside (**E**) the system constrain the system delivering its purpose to beneficiaries? With what consequences for whom? Also what constraints are applied, by whom, to the decision-makers by resource controllers inside the system to ensure that the beneficiaries really do benefit and the purpose fulfilled?

'Ought' mode questions:

- Who is influencing the system and its **D**ecision-making?

- Who ought to make the key **D**ecisions related to this purpose and the intended beneficiaries?

- What **R**esources ought to be available to the decision-makers to ensure that the beneficiaries benefit, and the purpose fulfilled?

- What constraints (**E**) ought to be applied, and by whom, to the decision-makers to ensure that the beneficiaries really do benefit and the purpose fulfilled? Also what constraints ought to be applied, and by whom, to the decision-makers by resource controllers inside the system to ensure that the beneficiaries really do benefit and the purpose fulfilled?

Critique of the 'is' from the position of the 'ought':

- What further comments do you have when comparing the 'is' with the 'ought'?

Knowledge and experts

So far we have discussed the two boundary choices linked to purpose (**P**) and resources (R). Let's add a third one, linked to knowledge (**K**), where the design concern is whether appropriate knowledge for a good intervention design and its *implementation* is available. In many cases this knowledge or expertise is provided by experts (**X**) that are hired by the decision-maker (who, of course, may also play an expert role). But take care, what do we mean by 'expert'? How do we, you, define expert? How do you judge the relevance of their expertise? It's not just a question of whether an expert has adequate expertise, but whether

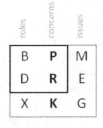

the right expert roles are involved. Who we regard as experts and how we judge their expertise is based on deep seated values. Should workers in a company be involved in decisions about investment decisions? Should parents be involved in decisions about their children's education? If so, what assumptions are we making about the value of their expertise? What risks are we taking that their expertise may be unhelpful or even harmful? During the design work it may become apparent that there is a need for additional expertise or knowledge. Will that be allowed? And what knowledge could that be? Is the expert allowed to stay silent if he or she notices serious implementation issues that are not in his or her terms of reference? Finally and ideally, a sound and healthy decision-making body (e.g., a donor for international development) would take it as a moral obligation to ensure that the planned-for improvement will be *appropriately informed*. When designing an intervention we seek to deal with these issues so that 'success' can be guaranteed. Thus, the third boundary critique is known as the guarantor (**G**), and the task is to avoid the fate of relying on guarantors that turn out to provide false guarantees.

Some questions to help this critique include:

'Is' mode questions:

- To what extent is the necessary **K**nowledge and expertise present for the system to deliver the purpose to the beneficiaries within the controls possessed by the decision-makers and the environmental constraints? (&**X**)

'Ought' mode questions:

- What **K**nowledge and expertise ought to be honoured and not marginalised? (&**X**)

- Given the uncertainties of the environment, what **G**uarantees ought to be used to provide assurance of effective implementation of the intervention (e.g., scientific advice, public consent, moral certitude)?

Critique of the 'is' from the position of the 'ought':

- What further comments do you have when comparing the 'is' with the 'ought'?

Legitimacy and witnessses

The first nine categories are focused on concerns and roles that are *involved* in or with the system: beneficiaries, decision-makers, experts all lie *within* the system and things that lie outside the system (like some aspects of measurement, resource constraints and guarantee of knowledge application) closely interrelate with things that are inside the system. The last three categories concern those who are *outside* our system but are *affected* by it. The key concern here is that of legitimacy (**L**). A system cannot legitimise itself: its legitimacy is decided by those outside the system. Yet legitimacy is essential for the system to operate ethically, morally and, as we illustrated earlier, pragmatically. In real terms an intervention cannot operate, no matter how strong the purpose, how well the resources are used and with all the correct expertise if it does not have the support in some way of those who may be affected in some way by the intervention. This influence may be direct or indirect.

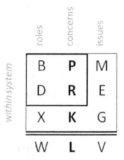

One of the main drivers of legitimacy is how a system handles interests (people or things) that are *negatively affected, marginalised or victimised* in some way by it. Any assessment of the values (purpose), power (resources), and expertise (knowledge) associated with any system will always be biased in some way towards promoting certain worldviews and marginalising other worldviews. That raises questions of legitimacy and moral authority. In other words, if your system (or intervention) is looked at from a different, opposing viewpoint, in what ways might your system's activities be considered as marginalising or victimising particular interests? How might your system be considered by those outside your system as coercive or evil rather than emancipatory or good? Who or what interest groups are likely to be the "victims" of the system, and, importantly, what type of representation ought to be made on their behalf? That is, who is capable of making representations on the victims' behalf, and on what basis would they make this claim?

It is the activist or witness (**W**) who takes it as his or her obligation to voice these concerns and who seeks to hold the system accountable for those consequences, possibly also with regard to compensating or accommodating the interests of the victims. Lack of legitimacy is a design flaw linked often to the unstated world views (**V**) of the system designers (i.e., you and us). On the positive side, arguments over legitimacy often expose these different worldviews and allow the development of approaches that can accommodate these world views while maintaining the overall purpose and beneficiaries. In other words, how might the underlying worldview associated with *your* system be reconciled with these opposing worldviews? Where might representation of opposing views be expressed, and what action ought to happen as a result?

At this stage you may be feeling somewhat puzzled or uncomfortable. This stage questions your moral or professional authority to say that what you think ought to be done is the right thing to do.

Why, you might ask, should I be interested in those affected by my system who may oppose what I am proposing? Are you leading me towards some bland, unworkable, unsustainable compromise that tries to satisfy everyone and pleases no one?

No, we are not asking you to do that or seeking that outcome.

We are saying that you need to consider these matters for ethical, political and practical reasons. The ethical reason is that wherever possible — as part of human society — you should aim to do as little harm as possible, even towards those who may be against what you are trying to do. The political reason is essentially about power — the more people whose interests you marginalise the less power you have to claim for the 'rightness' of your actions from a wider constituency, who, whether you like it or not, allow you to do your job. The practical reason may well be a consequence of your ethical and political decisions. Those who you exclude may fight back and perhaps destroy what you are trying to do. The more you consider those you are marginalising, the more you seek to find ways of accommodating those actions, the more likely you are to succeed with your proposals. *The trick is to do this without abandoning your own values or undermining your professional credibility.*

You might also not like some of the words we use, in particular 'victim' and 'marginalise', and especially the idea of deliberately choosing them. We also have used softer words like 'negatively affected' or 'disadvantaged'. But 'victim' and 'marginalise' are more effective ways to identify the moral boundaries you are constructing and force you to think about what you value — and that's the point of this systemic process.

So the final set of boundary deliberations is tough but necessary. In the questions below, note that the first half of the questions tend to be focused on the 'is' mode, and the latter questions tend to emphasise the 'ought' mode. But not as clearly as before because the job here is to deliberate on the 'is' and the 'ought' in more unified terms. However, in your own work feel free to play with the 'is' and 'ought' in ways that you think makes sense to you.

- In what way are the key role players (e.g., decision-makers, experts) not living up to their obligations to focus on the purpose to deliver the stated benefits to the intended beneficiaries?

- What is preventing key role players not living up to their obligations?

- Who or what is harmed by or is a victim of this system? How? (**L**)

- Compensated, how? (**L**)

- To what extent does that harm challenge or undermine the **L**egitimacy of the stated purpose of the system and how ought the system respond ethically to that challenge?

- Who ought to represent the interest of the harmed and how ought they be meaningfully involved in any deliberations about the system? (**W**)

- What 'world **V**iew' prevents the mitigation or compensation of those negatively affected by the system?

- What are the practical, ethical or moral consequences of taking this world **V**iew that might ultimately affect the ability of the system to deliver the benefits that are implied in its purpose?

- What alterations to this world **V**iew can minimise these negative effects? How can these alterations be incorporated into or allow to modify the system (by modifying the purpose, beneficiaries, decision-makers, system and environmental constraints, required expertise or guarantors)?

Putting the Boundary Critique into Practice

So how do you actually do all this?

The next sections divide the task into 3 steps:

Step One: Re-exploring the Rich Picture

Step Two: Outlining the Ideal Situation

Step Three: Boundary Critique of the Is and Ought

Step 1: Re-exploring the rich picture

That's an awful lot to absorb in one go, so it's a good idea to get everything in order before stepping out. So before getting into gear for the boundary critique, let's first look at the rich picture we made earlier and see what useful ideas for change are hidden in it. Some of these ideas will be used in the boundary critique.

Our case

This is a good point for us to go back to our rich picture to explore what *is* currently going on and what *ought* to be going on as a result of our intervention.

1.   **Pump irrigation:** The farmers and their families live in villages along the river. They work in association to grow rice in so-called village irrigation schemes, but they are not an egalitarian bunch. A key question is what value can be produced for the poorest and most marginalised? A central pump lifts the water from the river into the canals. The pump costs money for depreciation, fuel, financing and maintenance. The costs of the pump typically amount to one-third or half of the value of the crop produced with it. This does not leave enough for food security and income generation. Clearly, the situation would improve a lot if the pumping costs could  be reduced. Crop yield has a similar effect, as does water use efficiency or increasing the number of irrigation schemes per village. Not all of these are equally feasible. And who's to decide?

2.   **Crop marketing:** In the same picture above we see a truck bringing part of the produce to the market for consumers outside the village. This could be seen as a service by traders to the farmers or as a way for traders to make disproportionate profits to the detriment of the farmers. The question is: how can farmers get their fair share of the market price? And what's a fair share?

3.   **Pump origin:** In the right part of the rich picture we see equipment can be of Western or Asian origin. Equipment of Asian origin is a fraction of the cost of that of Western origin, but less reliable. It works well in Asia, though: without it millions of small-scale irrigation schemes would not have been there. Moreover, highly affordable pumps of the right design from China have an 80% market share in the Australian market, where they are combined with Western engines. The chances are that this approach could work in West Africa with a potential pumping cost reduction in the order of 50%. Current import channels may resist change.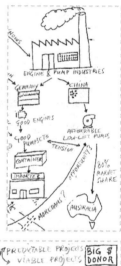

4.   **Intervention logic:** Similar to the risk-return trade-off in business, there is a viability-predictability trade-off in development intervention design, at least from the donor perspective. Predictability is about control, whereas viability is about fostering entrepreneurship (among farmers or private sector actors), which in 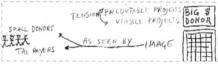 turn is about finding the right balance between risk and return. So the two types of trade-off are intertwined. The image or perception of donor effectiveness with the Western public presents a further complication. NGOs that execute donor projects or programmes may face a similar trade-off. The trouble is that often predictability is favoured, resulting in intervention design being heavily biased towards the project mode of operation as it gives the most control.

5.   **Value proposition:** It is increasingly recognised that NGOs should take the utmost care to develop good value propositions for the beneficiaries they are serving. If the proposition is good, farmers — or other clients — will respond favourably and aid effectiveness will ensue. NGOs may face several hindrances to formulating better value propositions, including the fact that they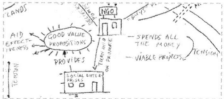

themselves often cannot operate in a more entrepreneurial manner, or their mission may not reflect the need for economic viability. Where rural services are concerned, a good value proposition is not just about cost-efficiency, but refers to matching each of the 4Ps (the marketing mix: price, product, place and promotion) against the farmers' needs.

6.   **Government:** The national government — in the bottom left of the rich picture — has an impact on what is generally considered the environment of the intervention. It can improve the business climate or protect certain businesses, it can exempt irrigation equipment from import duties, it can approve upstream developments that have a negative impact on that river hydrology, and it can demand measures to mitigate it. It controls food prices by allowing more or fewer grain imports. This is crucial, both for the urban and rural poor. Governments may also demand donors to design interventions that reduce aid dependency, rather than increasing it.

Your Task

Return to your rich picture and, like us, describe the key points that you observe.

TEAMWORK

Step 2: Outline of the ideal situation

Unless you start with the ideal you'll get something far less.

Author unknown

The 'ought' mode is used to describe the state of the situation as you'd like to see it — as it ought to be. It could be how it ought to be right now, or perhaps in the future. Yes, of course it is based on your values, or those with whom you are working. Indeed that's the point. You are going to progressively critique your view of what ought to happen based on the framings you've just developed. And we are going to do the same with our own example.

> **Ideal mapping** serves to identify the 'ought', the 'vision' of where we *want* to go in 5–10 years or so. It contrasts with *descriptive mapping*, which serves to identify the 'is', the current situation from where we must start.

Staying in an 'ought' mode is more difficult than it seems. It is surprisingly easy to refer back to how things are in general rather than as a specific ought to be, and once you do refer back you have lost analytical and critical power. So here's a trick to keep in these two modes. Take a piece of card or paper or open a new document and write the following on it:

Welcome to the year 2*,**
where 2*** is at least five
years ahead of this year.

Now put down your tablet, turn off your screen, and leave the room. Put on some coffee. Go for a walk. Talk to your bank manager. Take a shower. If there is a group of you, go to lunch, play a game of soccer. In fact do pretty much anything that will stop you thinking about the situation or the problem you are dealing with.

On your return, look at the year you'd written and imagine that everything about the situation has worked out as you think it should have. Or if you are part of a team doing this, everything as you collectively think it should have. Note this is not "will have happened" but "ought to have happened". And yes of course it is just your view (or you and your colleague's view) but remember you are the ones in this exercise with the power to select the boundaries. This is your redesign, your wicked solution that we are helping you critique here.

Now jot down very quickly the basic components of the situation in 2***. Perhaps the best way is to write individual aspects on Post-It notes and stick them to the wall or on a big sheet of paper. In fact this is exactly what we did with our case example.

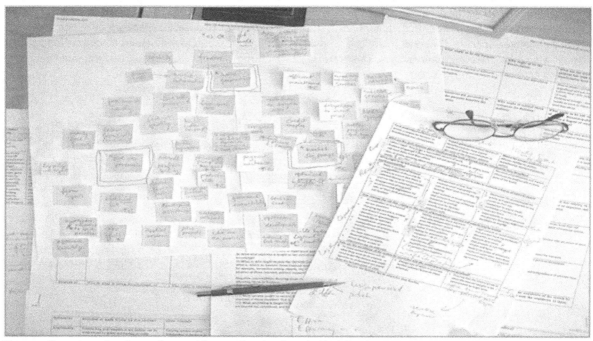

Figure 3.9 You may use Post-It notes for organising your thoughts about the ideal situation

It is important to keep in mind the framings you developed earlier in Section 3.2. It really is helpful if you construct three scenario, one based on each of the three 'framings'. That was how we originally wrote this case study, but it proved to be too complicated to express in the form of a workbook. Instead we constructed a single scenario *informed* by each of these three framings. It is an example of what we stated at the beginning; there is no recipe. Follow the principles but play around with the practice.

To repeat ourselves, do not consider how you think the situation might be, or what might be possible. Consider instead how it *ought* to be. This is the basis of keeping in the 'ought' frame of mind. Don't forget to look at your rich picture for inspiration. Indeed you are to some extent creating a rich picture of how things ought to be rather than as they are.

Our case

In our pump example, the problematic situation we are trying to resolve could be formulated as follows: Improve current smallholder irrigation development practice, which lacks effectiveness because of (1) the impossibility to renew the pumps when they wear out, and (2) the injustice of demanding renewal of the current pumps with their high cost and inefficiency. The high cost not only complicates pump renewal, but leaves a much smaller margin for food supply and income, which is the main intervention goal.

In five or ten years' time, taking into account the three framings — **food production, income generation and market for pumps** — we decided the situation ought to be such that (1) all farmers or farmer groups can renew their irrigation pumps without external aid or subsidies, (2) all farmers or farmer groups will have access to the number of irrigation pumps they need for growing enough food for feeding their families and with a surplus to sell for other basic needs, (3) the rural (agricultural, mechanical, financial and marketing) services needed to make this possible are cost efficient and no longer dependent on external aid, and (4) the procurement and operation of the irrigation pumps are optimised in terms of cost, pump capacity range, efficiency and reliability.

Your task

Describe the problematic situation you are trying to resolve and indicate what the future situation should be like in five or ten years' time.

Step 3: Boundary critique of 'is' and 'ought'

Boundary identification and critique

So what does all this mean for our particular case? How will you identify key boundary issues and how can you critique them? And, further down the road, how may boundary choices result in a systemic intervention outline?

To answer these questions, we will step with you through this assessment in the four stages described earlier. As a memory jogger and to avoid getting lost, we've included the key questions and repeated the basic principles that underpin them.

However, although what follows is a rigorous and detailed boundary critique, it's long and we don't want you to get stuck in the weeds. So here is a very brief description of some of the main insights that we came up with. The list can be expanded by adding ideas from the detailed critique.

	Ideal ('ought')	Initial/actual ('is')
Purpose & beneficiaries	To lift the constraints on equipment renewal, food production and income generation in suitable areas by achieving self-sustaining growth of a responsive private sector serving smallholder farmers with effective demand in a mutually beneficial relationship.	Establishing a limited number of highly productive village irrigation schemes with the purpose of significantly increasing food security of the target population.
Resources & decision-makers	The key decisions are still taken by donors and development organisations, but a stronger role will be available much earlier in the programme for those stakeholders that will determine ultimate sustainability, viz. the farmers and esp. the private sector.	The key decisions are taken by donors and one or more local development agencies associated with them. This gives full control over implementation.
Knowledge & experts	The value proposition of the initial intervention is corrected by bringing in business expertise for enterprise development and technical and commercial expertise for pump selection.	Expertise is mostly provided in the form of agronomic and irrigation engineering knowledge in order for the irrigation schemes to be as highly productive as possible.
Legitimacy & witnesses	Donors are no longer allowed to get away with low-risk, low-sustainability interventions. A systemic sustainability and effectiveness assessment should be part of any new plan.	The main 'victims' are 'sustainability' and 'autonomous growth'. The first is supposedly dealt with, whereas the second is not considered in the design of the project.

Table 3.7: Overview of the main insights gained from the boundary critique on the next pages

Purpose and beneficiaries

The development of a system starts with some idea of 'purpose'. Since a purpose reflects embedded values associated with someone or some group, it is valid to ask, "Who should benefit from this purpose?" Identifying first the *purpose* of the system (i.e., what's at stake) should help to identify who the intended *beneficiaries* ought to be (i.e., what stakeholder roles are privileged). This in turn raises questions about how we will know whether the beneficiaries are really benefitting. In other words, what key issues arise in *measuring or observing the success* of how well we are securing some improvement to those beneficiaries (human or otherwise)?

'Is' mode questions:

- What transformation or significant change do we observe? This question helps you to look critically at the stated **P**urpose (see also next question).

- What implied **P**urpose best describes this change? Your answer is likely to reflect one of the framings, in one way or the other.

- To what wider agenda (and whose agenda) might this **P**urpose belong? Your answer is likely to provide a rationale for the way the 'is' mode is justified.

- Who or what are the **B**eneficiaries of this purpose?

'Ought' mode questions:

- What transformation or significant change do we desire? You may find possible answers by looking at the work you did for the rich picture and the framings.

- What **P**urpose best describes this change? Look at the framings! You may not want to describe this in a fairly open way, leaving sufficient options in subsequent planning parameters.

- What wider agenda (and whose agenda) might this **P**urpose belong? This question helps you identify support for 'ought' mode initiatives.

- Who or what ought to be the **B**eneficiaries of this purpose? You may find alternative or additional beneficiaries from those you identified for the same question in the 'is' mode.

Questions for both modes:

- Who benefits from and who is harmed by the system? This question asks you to conduct a benefit-cost mapping, which may help you identify alternative **B**eneficiaries.

- How robust are your arguments that these are the 'right' **B**eneficiaries? Strange as this may sound, it can be surprisingly tempting to pick the 'wrong' beneficiaries.

- Do some of those in influential positions have other **P**urposes (e.g., 'hidden agendas')? How should the implications be handled? Hidden agendas are best identified by 'unfolding' the benefit map.

- How can we know if the beneficiaries benefit; how 'is' and 'ought' this be identified and measured? There will be some **M**easures of success that we can identify and implement, but there will be some that for a variety of reasons cannot be adopted for political or cultural reasons, and thus are chosen to be outside the boundary. Some will always be outside the boundary because we have no way of implementing those measures. You will note that the **M**easures of success or indicators depend on what purpose you chose.

Critique of the 'is' from the position of the 'ought':

- What further comments do you have when comparing the 'is' with the 'ought'?

Our case

'Is' The key transformation in the 'is' mode is one of establishing a limited number of highly productive village irrigation schemes with the **P**urpose of significantly increasing food security of the target population. This is justified by a global agenda of food security as a basic human right. The targeted **B**eneficiaries are poor, food insecure farmers and their families owning and working plots in these irrigation schemes. More affluent, food secure farmers are not part of the specified target group and are not served. Indirectly, increased modern rice production by pump irrigation leads to additional demand for rural services, such as input supply, maintenance of pumping equipment and crop marketing. Key indicators (**M**) are linked to areas irrigated, crop yields and levels of food self-sufficiency.

'Ought' In contrast, the key transformation in the desired 'ought' mode is one of (**P**) achieving self-sustaining growth of a responsive private sector serving the farmers fairly in a mutually beneficial relationship. Growth of the smallholder irrigation sector as a whole can ensure serving all farmers with effective demand to satisfy their needs for food and pumps. No farmer groups are excluded: farmers will have access as long as they can ensure payment (and those who cannot may be regarded as potential victims — see later). Market segmentation of the beneficiaries and other marketing strategies will help reach more farmers. The leading role of the private sector in this growth will lift the constraints on equipment renewal, food production and income generation in entire areas. This is justified by a global agenda of aid effectiveness. It involves a major effort of enterprise development with the private sector becoming a primary **B**eneficiary or client. A key question is how to make sure that the interaction between farmers and the private sector is indeed mutually beneficial, especially because the private sector is in it for the profit and competition is scarce. Key indicators (**M**) are technical and economic efficiency, affordability (for farmers), profitability (for private sector) and prospects for pump renewal (for both).

Critique

Critique of the 'is' from the position of the 'ought'

B: Targeting farmers directly is not effective. The benefits to farmers are below optimum and not sustainable. Non-target group farmers are excluded. The private sector provides some services, but these services have not been optimised.

P: The goal of food security (Framing 1) is commendable, but it cannot be achieved directly, especially not on sustainable terms. Just food production or security is not enough. Farm households are also in need of monetary income (Framing 2). Without good rural services, farmers will not be able to cope (Framing 3). Special attention ought to be paid to the payment arrangements. Ideally, these are embedded in the rural services, preferably in a transparent manner. The utility of co-operative development training should be reconsidered.

M: Measurement is limited to efficient implementation needs and not looking at indicators for long-term sustainability. The absence of indicators for sustainability is the most striking, considering past records.

Critique of the 'ought' from the position of the 'is'

B: Aid funds should not be directed to the establishment of private sector provided rural services. Let the private sector take care of itself. The project mode of aid delivery in the 'is' mode is well targeted to (needy) farmers.

P: The establishment of better and cheaper rural services is too risky and difficult. Only historical figures are available about non-renewal of pumping equipment. Better training will likely show that renewal rates are well up from historical records. Income generation from crop marketing should be limited to a minimum (i.e., the amount needed to pay for the various pumping costs and not beyond that, because marketing in these areas is difficult).

M: It is possible to measure the efficiency (i.e., cost) of private sector provided services before project withdrawal, but not withdrawal. So measurements are meaningless for long-term sustainability.

OK, time for you to do some work and fill out table 3.7.

Your case: Purpose and beneficiaries

TEAMWORK

Is:

Ought:

Is vs. Ought:

Ought vs. Is

Table 3.8: Template for critiquing impact-related boundary choices

Resources and decision-makers

Deliberating on matters of purpose and beneficiaries leads to questions regarding the *necessary resources* or *components* needed to ensure the beneficiaries benefit from the purpose. This will include people, money, things and intangibles, such as social capital. But who ought to be the *decision-makers* in control of such resources? There are, however, risks of having all the necessary resources under the control of those inside the system. If the decision-makers control all the resources, then there are no checks and balances[13] that would prevent the systems from being diverted from its purpose by other interests. The system cannot be controlled or held accountable in any way. In other words, a decision has to be made about how the resource managers can be kept in check and accountable. This in turn prompts questions as to what should be left *outside* the control of such decision makers.

Some questions that help critique these resource decision-making boundaries include:

'Is' mode questions:

- Who makes the key **D**ecisions related to this purpose and the beneficiaries? Who currently does this?

- What **R**esources are available to the decision-makers to ensure that the beneficiaries benefit and the purpose fulfilled?

- What things outside (**E**) the system constrain the system delivering its purpose to beneficiaries? With what consequences for whom. Also what constraints are applied, and by whom, to the decision-makers by resource controllers inside the system to ensure that the beneficiaries really do benefit and the purpose fulfilled?

'Ought' mode questions:

- Who is influencing the system and its **D**ecision-making?

- Who ought to make the key **D**ecisions related to this purpose and the intended beneficiaries?

- What **R**esources ought to be available to the decision-makers to ensure that the beneficiaries benefit, and the purpose fulfilled?

- What constraints (**E**) ought to be applied, and by whom, to the decision-makers to ensure that the beneficiaries really do benefit and the purpose fulfilled? Also what constraints ought to be applied, and by whom, to the decision-makers by resource controllers inside the system to ensure that the beneficiaries really do benefit and the purpose fulfilled?

Critique of the 'is' from the position of the 'ought':

- What further comments do you have when comparing the 'is' with the 'ought'?

13The notion of "checks and balances" points to the possibility of improving decision-making by reconfiguring control over resources among different key decision-makers. In the "ought" mode of the irrigation case this is done by changing control over the pumping equipment. This implies that control is not delegated to somebody outside the system but stays within the system.

Our case

'Is'   The key decisions are currently taken by donors and one or more local agencies associated with them. They can do so because they provide most of the resources (pumps, staff, funds). The donors typically decide to operate in project mode and retain key decisions to make sure local agencies have adequate human and financial resources to run the project and determine which farmers or villages participate. A western-biased tender system not only ensures favourable terms of procurement for the donor, but also ensures that only western manufacturers compete to determine the final choice of equipment. The pumping equipment is ceded to the farmers on very favourable terms (highly subsidised) or at no cost at all. Very limited efforts are made to involve the national or local private sector. Is the private sector excluded from being admitted as relevant decision-makers, simply because they are not part of a poor and insecure target group, or because it is assumed to be available and efficient? Due to difficulties of pump renewal, farmers who are being served now, may not be so in the near future. While the project is there it takes full responsibility for a hitch-free implementation and makes the necessary financial and human resources available. This stifles short-term criticism, but may reduce long-term viability.

'Ought'   In our 'ought' mode we believe the key decisions are still taken by donors and development organisations, but a stronger role will be available much earlier in the programme for those stakeholders that will determine ultimate sustainability, viz. the farmers and the private sector. The private sector will be responsible for the pumps — providing the farmers with access to them through a rental service — and their renewal, as well as other services, such as repair and maintenance, input supply, and marketing or transport. Some of these services may be combined and packaged or embedded. All this makes local and national business actors key decision-makers in their own right. It will be up to the donor to develop mechanisms that make sure the value of the private sector to the farmers is adequate and decide who initiates or stimulates efforts to optimise that value. The determination of the price for pumps must be influenced in favour of the farmers by stimulating competitive market forces in the economic 'environment'. Mechanisms to create such competition and yet avoid false competition between development organisations and the private sector must be developed. It is assumed that procurement of cost-effective (and therefore sufficiently reliable and maintainable) equipment can be arranged and that farmers on their own or with assistance from a third party will be able to maintain yields at an adequate level. There are signs that certain government officials will not allow sourcing equipment from Asia, because they are convinced of its inferiority. It may be difficult to ensure affordable cost of ownership of equipment, even with the relatively low prices of Asian equipment, considering that bank lending rates in West-African countries are excessively high. Considering the control of national government over key environmental factors, what demands can be made on government to open up decision-making and enable developmentally favourable ways for village irrigation development, e.g., with regard to upstream water diversion or custom duties on pumping equipment?

Critique

Critique of the 'is' from the position of the 'ought'

D: Habit, the need for accountability, and the possibility for greater control over implementation make the donor opt for the project mode of aid delivery instead of a more sustainability-oriented business mode.

R: Farmers are simply too poor to manage a relatively large revolving fund for pump renewal, so renewal ought to be ensured in another way. A system of annual payment (rental) seems much more feasible, especially if there is the threat of equipment being withdrawn in the case of default. Alternative procurement options must urgently be investigated.

E: In the 'is' mode, rural services are present, but they are not optimised or well co-ordinated. Due to high interest rates and high equipment costs, pump rental cannot come off the ground. Capital investment, especially in items that must be written off over longer periods, is very difficult.

Critique of the 'ought' from the position of the 'is'

D: It must be remembered that donor organisations are under the obligation of those who fund them to spend funds carefully. To ensure long-term maintenance, the Western origin of the equipment is undisputed. National importers are able to ensure spare-parts and mechanical expertise, which is not the case for Asian sourced equipment.

R: If the equipment is in the hands of the private sector, they may take it away from the farmers on arbitrary grounds, e.g., to provide it to higher bidders.

E: Rural enterprises must join forces with donors and national importers to seek a long-term solution to the problem of high interest rates. Ceding the equipment to farmers at low or no cost is most certainly an effective approach.

Your case: Resources and decision-makers

TEAMWORK

Is:

Ought:

Is vs. Ought:

Ought vs. Is

Table 3.9: Template for critiquing control-related boundary choices

Knowledge and experts

We now have greater clarity of purpose, beneficiaries and aspects of the decision-making process. But that is not enough. How do we ensure that the necessary use of resources are good use of resources? For that we require information, knowledge and skills. So what ought to be the necessary types and levels of knowledge and skill to ensure that the system actually has practical applicability and works towards its purpose within the decision-making environment? Who ought to provide such expertise? To what extent should those people also play a decision-making role, or should they be more independent? More importantly is our reliance on the expertise of experts wise? Expertise provides some guarantee of success, but are we accessing the most appropriate expertise? Are we setting the system up to fail? Is the guarantee a false one; relying on experts or expertise that may turn out to be unwise or misleading?

Some questions that will help identify and critique these knowledge-based boundary choices:

'Is' mode questions:

- To what extent is the necessary **K**nowledge and expertise present for the system to deliver the purpose to the beneficiaries within the controls possessed by the decision-makers and the environmental constraints? (&**X**)

'Ought' mode questions:

- What **K**nowledge and expertise ought to be honoured and not marginalised? (&**X**)
- Given the uncertainties of the environment, what **G**uarantees ought to be used to provide assurance of effective implementation of the intervention (e.g., scientific advice, public consent, moral certitude)?

Critique of the 'is' from the position of the 'ought':

- What further comments do you have when comparing the 'is' with the 'ought'?

Our Case

'Is'   In the 'is' situation, expertise is mostly provided in the form of agronomic and irrigation engineering knowledge in order for the irrigation schemes to be highly productive. Close supervision (a guarantor) ensures that technical advice is applied to the letter and wherever else farmers fail to operate with efficiency and efficacy. The project format has been time-tested, but mostly for guaranteed and timely short-term results only. There is a one-sided reliance on expertise that fits with the project-mode of intervention rather than the enterprise-mode of intervention. These types of approaches and knowledge may provide a false guarantee of project success. The need for knowledge to improve the value proposition under low-supervision conditions is ignored. Pump selection expertise is held mostly by the manufacturers asked to participate in the donor's tender-for-bid system. This guarantees reliability, but it does so at considerable cost both to the farmers, directly, and to the long-term viability of the intervention.

'Ought'   In the 'ought' mode the value proposition can be corrected by bringing in business expertise for enterprise development and technical and commercial expertise for pump selection. The focus is shifted from short-term results in project mode to long-term effectiveness in business mode. Guarantees must be built in for low-supervision conditions that will occur after donor withdrawal. This applies to crop yields as well as the pricing regime of rural services. In the case of crop yields this means that the prospects of smallholder irrigation viability at, say, 60% of the supervised yield levels should be explored. At the same time, efforts ought to be made to see if unsupervised yields cannot be increased somehow. Such efforts are not cost- and risk-free, which requires higher levels of leniency and transparency about the levels of uncertainty associated with sustainability, because that is the only way to ensure the necessary learning takes place. An 'ought' type of intervention cannot be planned as well as an 'is' type. One could also say that all this does not imply that 'ought' interventions are inherently more risky, but rather that the risks are distributed differently. In the 'is' mode, risks are pushed over the edge of the time horizon of the project, whereas in the 'ought' mode they are faced squarely during implementation.

Critique

Critique of the 'is' from the position of the 'ought'

X: It is clear that the 'is' mode of intervention has a technocratic bias in the choice of experts as opposed to a more balanced mix of technology, organisation and entrepreneurship in the 'ought' mode. Some knowledge becomes available only during implementation. This means experts must make sure that people are equipped to do the necessary learning along the way.

K: The focus on high yields using agronomist masks looming environmental sustainability issues. It is doubtful that the right expertise for pump optimisation can be incorporated in the tendering process. Therefore, alternative forms of procurement must be used that enable the use of other forms of knowledge. In this example the knowledge seems to be available in Australia rather than in Europe.

G: The guarantees that are provided are all associated with the technology transfer model. A more balanced approach would involve the local and national private sector.

Critique of the 'ought' from the position of the 'is'

X: It is very difficult to plan for 'real' learning. And if there is learning, it is not easy to guarantee that the necessary resources are available, especially if there is a lot of risk or if it is uncertain how to assess the level of risk involved. Generally, the experiences with rural service creation, although necessary, are mixed at best. As usual, we find ourselves between a rock and a hard place. So the first requirement is not to get crushed.

K: Secure implementation can only be guaranteed in project mode with close supervision. Lower yields are simply not feasible.

G: There must be sufficient guarantees that the business approach can work, or else the project model is much preferable. Close supervision is hard to replace by embedded ones, because they are expensive.

Your case: Knowledge and experts

Is:

Ought:

Is vs. Ought:

Ought vs. Is

Table 3.10: Template for critiquing knowledge-related boundary choices

Moral authority and world view — protecting the affected

You will recall from earlier stages in this book that there were three reasons why it is important to critique your boundaries: ethical, political and pragmatic. Deliberation on these issues is critical to the feasibility of your planned intervention.

The three steps we have just climbed are concerned with those directly *involved* in the system: the beneficiaries, the decision-makers, the experts. However, any assessment of the values (motivation), power (control) and expertise (knowledge) associated with any system will always be biased in some way towards promoting certain worldviews and marginalising other worldviews. That raises questions of legitimacy and moral authority. In other words, if your system is looked at from a different, opposing viewpoint, in what ways might your system's activities be considered as marginalising or victimising particular interests? How might your system be considered by those outside your system as coercive or evil rather than emancipatory or good? Who or what interest groups are likely to be the 'victims' of the system, and, importantly, what type of representation ought to be made on their behalf? That is, who is capable of making representations on the victims' behalf, and on what basis would they make this claim? Finally, how might the underlying worldview associated with *your* system be reconciled with these opposing worldviews? Where might representation of opposing views be expressed, and what action ought to happen as a result?

- In what way are the key role players (e.g., decision-makers, experts) not living up to their obligations to focus on the purpose to deliver the stated benefits to the intended beneficiaries?
- What is preventing key role players not living up to their obligations?
- Who or what is harmed by, or is a victim of this system? How? (**L**)
- Compensated, how? (**L**)
- To what extent does that harm challenge or undermine the **L**egitimacy of the stated purpose of the system and how ought the system respond ethically to that challenge?
- Who ought to represent the interest of the harmed and how ought they be meaningfully involved in any deliberations about the system? (**W**)
- What 'world **V**iew' prevents the mitigation or compensation of those negatively affected by the system?
- What are the practical, ethical or moral consequences of taking this world **V**iew that might ultimately affect the ability of the system to deliver the benefits that are implied in its purpose?
- What alterations to this world **V**iew can minimise these negative effects? How can these alterations be incorporated into, or allow to modify the system (by modifying the purpose, beneficiaries, decision-makers, system and environmental constraints, required expertise or guarantors)?

Our case

'Is'   The main 'victims' in the 'is' approach are 'sustainability' and 'autonomous growth', which are considered to be beyond the control of the project. There is considerable fall-out for various groups, including unserved farmers that are not part of the target group, national importers and Asian manufacturers that are side-lined in favour of direct procurement from Western producers, targeted farmers that are unable or incapable of renewal when the time comes. Even if the Western tax payer loses, the donor seems to operate on the basis that it can be ignored, as long as there are no development 'scandals' breaking out. The donor worldview that drives this situation is one of the poor as aid recipients that are to be reached by donor-driven projects. The farmers themselves perceive it as having good or bad luck. Donors tend to suppose that by procuring directly from the West, they are giving the taxpayer the biggest possible bang for their buck. The government angle is that the project is one of many moderately or marginally successful efforts towards improving national food security. It may therefore decide to divert upstream water at the cost of downstream development. Local politicians may prefer continued aid dependence because it helps them get re-elected if they can secure new waves of pumps from other donors.

'Ought'   In the 'ought' model of development, Western exporters will be side-lined if more non-Western producers supply pumps that are of equal quality and thus pose no risk to the farmers. The wider public must have access to timely and objective information by transparent reporting. Donors cannot be allowed to get away with low-risk, but at the same time low-sustainability interventions. Local politicians must take pride in helping to strengthen a business model that works, rather than lobbying for successive waves of free pumps. What possibilities are there to avoid or fight the bias in donor decision-making as a result of private-sector lobbies? There is the notion that cheap Asian manufacturers are much less reliable than more costly Western ones. A middle way would be to use all-Asian equipment with the exception of Western engines. This would open the way to working with national equipment importers, whose mainstay is the import of equipment with engines of a single European make.

Critique

Critique of the 'is' from the position of the 'ought'

W: To have no 'scandals' is too low an ambition for donors. The tax payer deserves real, not tokenist development. There is ample scope for exploring alternative options that have a much higher potential for sustainability. Donors could give more leeway to evaluators to bring out such alternatives and to inquire more deeply into the initial and evolving rationales of project designs. International development is a knowledge-intensive sector and must therefore be treated as such.

L: Side-lining of key private sector actors augurs badly for sustainability. Opportunities for competitive involvement of private businesses have to be explored. In the end — that is, after the withdrawal of aid — only businesses can provide farmers with the services they need. It is unacceptable that groups of farmers are excluded as the result of a target group approach. If food is a human right, then all farmers should have equal access to pumps.

V: It must be admitted that only a limited number of poor can be reached by donor projects. Development must in the end have the capacity for self-sustained growth or it will be to no avail. The absence of development 'scandals' is in itself not a good sign.

Critique of the 'ought' from the position of the 'is'

W: Projects are conceived in the best possible way. If they have flaws it is because there is simply no better way of doing things. If a very experienced donor with well-paid experts doesn't know best, who does?

L: Only Western exporters are reliable. Exporters from elsewhere simply should get their exporting act together. As soon as they do, they will be allowed to participate in the tendering system.

V: If farming becomes a business and the private sector the provider of services, the poorest stand to lose. The private sector will always manoeuvre itself into a position where it profits optimally, if not from donors, then from farmers.

Your case: Legitimacy and world view

Is:

| |
| |

TEAMWORK

Ought:

| |
| |

Is vs. Ought:

| |
| |

Ought vs. Is

| |
| |

Table 3.11 Template for critiquing legitimacy-related boundaries

Summary of Boundaries: critique for impact

The aim of focusing on boundaries is to help make practical and ethical decisions about the wicked problem so that your attempt to intervene is justified and can be seen as legitimate and moral. You will do this by first identifying four critical boundary decisions made by any design or intervention — purpose, control of resources, notions of expertise, and the ideology or world view that underpins your design or intervention. You then subjected these choices to a critique by comparing what currently 'is' and what you believe 'ought' to be those decisions. On the basis of that critique you make the necessary boundary choices that provide the ingredients for your final intervention design.

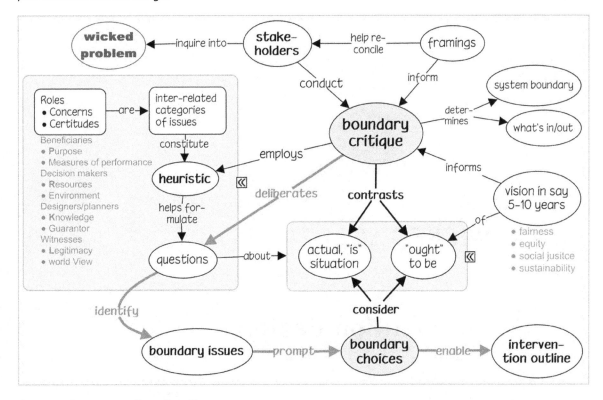

Figure 3.10: Concept map of boundary critique

WICKED SOLUTIONS

Intervention design

Innovative corrective action

Two roads diverged in a wood, and I —
I took the one less travelled by,
And that has made all the difference.

Robert Frost

Systemic intervention outline

So we've picked apart the problem to its bones, although in doing so we've used scenarios (e.g., the 'ought' mode) that imply solutions. But now it's time for some real 'solutions' inasmuch as wicked problems can have solutions. We can't put this off any longer.

> If you've got here straight from Level 1 or Level 2, take a look at the Glossary at the end of the book to catch up with some of the jargon developed in Level 3.

Ideally, of course, we'd work up the 'ought' scenario into a feasible solution. However, this may not be possible; perhaps it poses too much of a challenge to the current value system and just builds resistance, or that legitimacy evades that solution. Or because it poses practical or strategic problems. Many of these feasibility issues have been brought up during the critique. Whether they did or not depended on your systemic sensitivity[14] and your willingness or ability to see the situation through the eyes of others. So to address these issues we propose a series of steps, designed to make the best possible use of the boundary critique results. This may sound obvious, but not all of us have the cognitive capacity to juggle fifty or more critical insights simultaneously. We certainly don't.

> **Outline of a process for innovative intervention design**
> 1. Use Post-Its for a full overview of the critique.
> 2. Summarise the key points of the "ought" situation for the questions relating to purpose, resources, knowledge and legitimacy.
> 3. Finalise your **intervention design** to improve its overall feasibility. This may involve your sound judgment for organisational or management design measures to make the intervention practical.

But remember that this will be your idea of what might be feasible and right. Given the wickedness of the situation it is the best you can do.

---

[14] There are many ways to enhance your systemic sensibility. 'Look for higher leverage points' is one of the system guidelines formulated by Kauffman (1980). Meadows (1997) identified 12 levels for systemic leverage, in increasing order of effectiveness and resistance (or difficulty of implementation or acceptance): numbers, buffers, stock and flow structures, delays, balancing loops, reinforcing loops, information flows, rules, self-organisation, goals, paradigms and transcending paradigms.

Our wicked solution

1. Post-It overview of the critique

Fig. 4.1. You may use Post-Its to keep an overview of all your critical insights.

2. Key points from the critique

Purpose   The key transformation in the 'ought' mode is to lift the constraints on equipment renewal, food production and income generation at a large enough scale for achieving self-sustaining growth of a responsive private sector serving smallholder farmers empowered to exercise effective demand in a mutually beneficial relationship with that private sector.

> *'Ought' critique of 'is'   The goal of food security may be commendable, but targeting farmers directly is not sustainable. Target group farmers are not served well, while non-target group farmers are not served at all. The private sector provides some services, but these services are far from optimised. Special attention ought to be paid to the payment arrangements. Ideally, these are embedded in the rural services. Farm households need cash income as well as food. Co-operative development training is irrelevant. Indicators for sustainability are lacking.*

> *'Is' critique of 'ought'   Care should be taken not to pamper the private sector with aid funds. Or else, the project mode of aid delivery directly to (poor) farm households in the old situation may be preferable, provided training is improved. The establishment of better and cheaper rural services is not an easy task. Income generation may also not be so easy: crop marketing in remote rural areas is difficult. In the end it may be just as difficult to create a sustainable solution with private sector involvement as without.*

Resources   In our 'ought' mode, we believe the key decisions are still taken by donors and development organisations, but a stronger role will be available much earlier in the programme for those stakeholders that will determine ultimate sustainability and effectiveness, viz. the farmers and the private sector.

'Ought' critique of 'is'   *Habit, the need for accountability, and the possibility for greater control over implementation make the donor opt for the project mode of aid delivery instead of a more sustainability-oriented business mode. Unfortunately, the donor ignores the fact that farmers are simply too poor to manage a relatively large revolving fund for pump renewal. A rental system seems much more feasible, especially if there is the threat of equipment being withdrawn in the case of default. Due to high interest rates and high equipment costs, pump rental cannot come off the ground. Capital investment, especially in items that must be written off over longer periods, is very difficult. Equipment of Asian origin would lower costs significantly.*

'Is' critique of 'ought'   *To ensure long-term maintenance of equipment, the Western origin of the equipment is undisputed. National importers are able to ensure spare-parts and mechanical expertise, which is not the case for Asian sourced equipment. If the equipment is in the hands of the private sector, they may take it away from the farmers on arbitrary grounds, e.g., to provide it to higher bidders. Rural enterprises must join forces with donors and national importers to seek a solution to the problem of high interest rates or else giving pumps away is better.*

Knowledge   In the 'ought' mode, the value proposition of the intervention is corrected by bringing in business expertise for enterprise development and technical and commercial expertise for pump selection and procurement.

'Ought' critique of 'is'   *The 'is' mode of intervention has a technocratic bias in the choice of experts as opposed to a more balanced mix of technology, organisation and entrepreneurship in the 'ought' mode. Some knowledge becomes available only during implementation, so experts must ensure that people will learn along the way. The focus on high yields using agronomist stifles criticism of the approach. The right expertise for pump optimisation can only be found in Australia and Asia rather than in Europe. The 'is' guarantees are all associated with the technology transfer model of development. A more balanced approach would involve the local and national private sector.*

'Is' critique of 'ought'   *It is very difficult to plan for 'real' learning. Generally, the experiences with rural service creation, although necessary, are mixed at best. Secure implementation can only be guaranteed in project mode with close supervision. Lower yields are simply not feasible. Forms of close supervision are hard to replace by external or embedded ones, because they may not be around or are simply expensive. There must be sufficient guarantees that the business approach can work, or else the project mode is preferable.*

Legitimacy   In the 'ought' model of development, donors acknowledge that they can no longer support risk-avoiding interventions that entail low sustainability.

'Ought' critique of 'is'   *The Western tax payer deserves real, not tokenistic development. To have no 'scandals' is too low an ambition for donors. Development must in the end have the capacity for self-sustained growth or it will be to no avail. The absence of development 'scandals' is in itself not a good sign. Opportunities for competitive involvement of private businesses have to be explored. In the end — that is, after the withdrawal of aid — only businesses can provide farmers with the services they need. It is unacceptable that groups of farmers are excluded as the result of a target group approach. If food is a human right, then all farmers should have equal and adequate access to pumps.*

'Is' critique of 'ought'   *Projects are conceived in the best possible way. If they have flaws it is because there is simply no better way of doing things. If a very experienced donor with well-paid experts doesn't know best, who does? Only Western exporters are reliable. Exporters from elsewhere simply should get their exporting act together. As soon as they do, they will be allowed to participate in the tendering system. If farming becomes a business and the private sector the provider of services, the poorest stand to lose. The private sector will always manoeuvre itself into a position where it maximises profits, if not from donors, then from farmers.*

3. Outline of the intervention design

The final design is a synthesis of the ideas generated by the critique. To make the design practical and feasible some additional ideas had to be added. To repeat ourselves, this is our idea of what might be feasible or right.

Purpose and beneficiaries   The purpose is to lift the constraints on equipment renewal, food production and income generation by achieving self-sustaining growth of a responsive private sector. The direct beneficiary is the private sector with the smallholder irrigation farmers as its clients. The private sector beneficiaries are: (a) international equipment sellers from Europe (engines) and Asia (pumping equipment); (b) national equipment importers and dealers in Sahelian countries; (c) local pump rental and credit systems to serve the farmers; and (d) other local enterprises to provide various services to farmers, e.g., for input supply, pump maintenance and repair, transport and marketing.

Resources and decision-making   A new actor will be established by the donor to provide the above chain of private sector beneficiaries with the necessary co-ordination to become responsive to the farmer needs and make a fair profit serving them. This new co-ordination centre (CC) for smallholder irrigation development will be a social enterprise. Once it has achieved a certain scale of operations it will no longer need external support or subsidies. Initially, the CC will have to invest in confidence building between the various stakeholders. The CC will also channel considerable financial resources in the form of low interest loans towards capital development of pumping equipment. To do so effectively it will help establish and supervise effective local pump rental and credit businesses. These local pump rental businesses will develop and manage a network of farmer groups and small local enterprises to serve these farmers. Reasonable assurances must be sought from government with regard to key environmental factors, such as large-scale upstream developments (that may deteriorate downstream hydrology), the level of custom duties on pumping equipment, and the national food policy, which affects the profitability of smallholder farming.

Knowledge and guarantors   During the initial phase, the CC will be an important provider of knowledge. Knowledge for the design and procurement of Asian pumping equipment (cost-efficiency, reliability), knowledge for ensuring adequate involvement of the private sector (incentives/lures, business plans, competitive price formation) and knowledge to establish appropriate payment arrangements for farmers or farmer groups (pump rental, inputs, long crop production and marketing cycles). Some of these ideas require some trial-and-error in the form of probes or pilots. This will also provide the time and occasion for ownership development among key stakeholders. A local project on a limited scale is fine temporarily to refine the intervention model, but from the start answers must be sought for supporting a national or regional approach. This is the only scale at which major private actors can be expected to be lured to participate with enthusiasm.

Legitimacy and worldview   The intervention is designed to address a deep concern about the failure of making pump-based, smallholder irrigation for food production along Sahelian rivers sustainable. In the old set-up everybody loses: Western tax payers, Sahelian farm families (both those who are served for some years and those who are not served at all, because of the limited scope of the original project), donors, and various private sector actors for not being able to develop a profitable market. In the new worldview, farmers are no longer aid dependent — because they rent pumps instead of receiving them as a gift — and the private sector is no longer bypassed because only enterprises, small and large, can keep the wheels of smallholder irrigation development turning.

Your wicked solution

1. Use Post-Its for a full overview of the critique.
2. Summarise the key points of the "ought" situation for the questions relating to purpose, resources, knowledge and legitimacy.
3. Finalise your **intervention design** to improve its overall feasibility. This may involve your sound judgment for organisational or management design measures to make the intervention practical.

Final check and — now what?

Without deviation from the norm, progress is not possible.

Frank Zappa

By now you should have a pretty solid start to addressing your wicked problem with a wicked solution. Of course it is still only a start — once you implement your intervention you will need to ensure you stay responsive and redesign when necessary. A systemic view, a systemic approach, is always incomplete. Action creates further information and further insights.

It's not essential to go through the entire process described in this book every time you want to change your design, but we hope by now that you'd agree that it is a good idea to keep an eye on the following issues:

TEAMWORK

1. How's the 'rich picture' looking? Do you want to add or subtract from it?
2. How are you now framing things? How do they relate to your original framings? How do any new ways of framing the situation improve your understanding and strategies?
3. What new boundary issues have arisen and how are you addressing them?

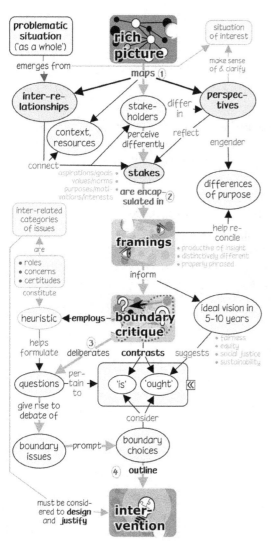

Figure 4.2: Summary of the last two sections

Summary of the last two sections

We readily admit that the deep dive of Level Three and the contents of the Intervention Design section can be confusing at first. So we are providing you with one more overview to help you make sense of it all, and of the book cover at the same time. Just follow the downward direction of the arrows, especially the fat ones. Encircled numbers mark the four steps.

Step 1 is to **map** the inter-relationships and perspectives. The inter-relationships connect the stakeholders, stakes, resources and environment. It is from the network of inter-relationships that the problematic situation emerges. The situation itself emerges within a wider, more general situation of interest. The stakeholder perspectives help to make sense of the situation of interest and clarify the meaning and importance of the problematic situation. It is best to work with a team of key stakeholders.

Step 2 is to **frame** the main perspectives. These framings can help to reconcile differences of purpose as a result of diverging perspectives. They are also important to inform an ideal vision of what you want to achieve in 5–10 years and help formulate the critical questions in the next step.

Step 3 is to **critique** (i.e., critically examine by discussing) the 'system' boundaries. The 'systems approach' aims at both systemic inquiry and design, so 'system' refers to both the problematic situation ('is') and the outcome of the systemic intervention ('ought' or its approximation). Use is made of a heuristic to formulate questions on 12 inter-related categories of issues that need to be considered for justifying your systemic interventions. If you find it difficult to make all the boundary choices or want to make sure strongly contrasting stakes are served adequately, we suggest you add one more step.

Step 4 is to **design** your systemic intervention. After you have summarised the key points of the "ought" situation for the questions relating to purpose, resources, knowledge and legitimacy, you can finalise your intervention design to improve its overall feasibility. A systemic view, a systemic approach, is always incomplete. Action creates further information and further insights, so you will need to ensure you stay responsive and redesign when necessary.

Expanding your ability to think systemically

A mind that is stretched by a new experience can never go back to its old dimensions.

Oliver Wendell Holmes, Jr.

You've come close to the end of the book. You've used the approaches we've described and want to learn more or go deeper. What are your options?

We wrote this book because we often saw people trying out methods drawn from the systems field but giving up half way through. Why? Two reasons.

Firstly, some systems methods appear simple conceptually, but in practice turn out to be rather more complicated than at first sight. You may have tried to repair a bicycle and found the same thing — that's why there are bicycle repair shops. We suspect that even your route through this book had its moments. We certainly had ours.

Secondly, it's not a good use of spanners to drive in nails. It works if you've nothing else at hand, but a hammer is a much more effective option. While all systems methods deal with inter-relationships, perspectives and boundaries; while all systems methods are focused on wicked problems, some are better at addressing different kinds of problem than others. It's going to be hard work if you've picked a method that's best at addressing inter-relationships yet your key task is exploring boundary choice.

Consequently, we've included a sample of systems methods you may have heard about and what we believe are their particular strengths. If you haven't heard of these methods and they look like something that would be useful to you, then check out the references in the Further Reading section at the end of this book.

Systems approaches especially good at exploring inter-relationships

System Dynamics is an approach that seeks to explore the consequences of non-linear relationships and delay. It is usually, although not always, used in conjunction with computer simulation. We often assume cause and effect relationships that are relatively sequential and linear: A leads to B leads to C. For example, we might understand that 'training' (A) leads to increased knowledge (B) which leads to employment in a particular specialism (C). Contrast system dynamics acknowledges that, in this example, A and B may feed off each other and that C may cause A to reduce. So training (A) might increase knowledge (B) and this knowledge may increase the demand for further training (A) which leads to greater knowledge (B). Or alternatively, knowledge (B) may lead to people gaining employment in the field (C), which might reduce their ability to engage in further training (A) that they need because they are now busy applying their knowledge. On top of this recursive behaviour there may be delays between 'cause' and 'effect' that further complicate the picture. So whilst training might affect knowledge quite quickly, knowledge may affect the demand for further training more slowly than gaining employment affects the demand for more training. Thus, whilst the capacity of the situation may be enhanced — at least initially (i.e., more training, knowledge, employment) — over time the capability of the situation reduces.

Viable System Modelling is based on the idea that different 'levels' within a situation need different kinds of information to function effectively. The model has five levels or 'systems':

System 1	The system of individual operational units within an organisation.
System 2	The system responsible for stability and resolving conflict between operational units.
System 3	The systems responsible for optimisation of, or generating synergy between operational units.
System 4	Organisation wide strategies and future plans. The means by which the organisation adapts to an external changing environment.
System 5	Policy development.

VSM[15] is commonly used to understand why monitoring and information management procedures are ineffective. An organisation's capacity is the sum total of all information possessed by an organisation. Each of the five systems needs information to function. However, not all of the information required by one system is generated inside that system — it makes demands on other systems for information. So each system is having to handle its own information needs, which it understands, and the information needs of other systems, which if doesn't understand and is often not motivated to ensure relevance and timeliness. So bad information sloshes around the organisation and thus its viability is threatened. Capacity does not match capability. VSM is thus used as a tool to help organisations balance capability and capacity and ensure that the right information is generated in the right place, supplied to the right people at the right time to allow them to take the right decisions.

Systems approaches especially good at exploring perspectives

Soft systems is a methodology that first forces you to consider alternative perspectives (e.g., development as 'aid', development as 'patronage', development as a 'tool of foreign policy', development as 'empowerment'). It then asks a series of questions that help you work out what the structure, function and logical consequences are of each perspective.

Of course 'reality' is always a mixture of perspectives. Soft systems do not force you to pick one perspective over the other, or even prioritise them. Instead, it encourages you to separate these perspectives, work out the implications of each and then assess how best to integrate them in a way that they work *for* rather than *against* each other.

Activity systems is an approach closely associated with the idea of communities of practice. A community of practice is a set of jointly mutually agreed and shared activities directed towards a common purpose. However, it is possible that, in reality, people can agree to a set of shared activities that are in fact directed towards different purposes. Activity systems approaches enable people to engage constructively in resolving the tensions that arise when circumstances expose the fact that people are engaged in the same activities but to different ends. So from a conventional capacity development perspective the focus might be on the quality of the actual counselling; an activity systems approach would be in developing the capability to handle conflict constructively.

Systems approaches especially good at critiquing boundary choice

The section of this book on boundary critique is based on *Critical Systems Heuristics*, perhaps the best known systems approach that challenges our choice of boundaries.

Systems approaches especially good at mapping situations

A method often associated with system dynamics is causal-loop diagramming, which is especially good at mapping situations. *Causal loop diagrams* are based on the notion of feedback loops; circular chains of 'cause' and 'effect' (although the distinction between these two notions are by definition rather unnecessary). The relationship between adjacent variables can be either positive (i.e., if A decreases, then B decreases), or negative (i.e., if A increases then B decreases). Loops with an odd number of negative relationships are known as balancing loops and with an even number of 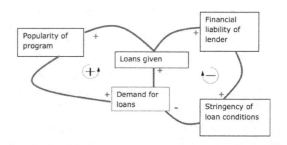 negative relationships as reinforcing loops. Above is an example that sought to understand why an economic development fund had huge swings in uptake[16].

15 Walker, J. An introduction to the Viable System Model as a diagnostic & design tool for co-operatives & federations, see http://www.esrad.org.uk/resources/vsmg_3/screen.php?page=1qguide (checked 19/5/14).

16 Systems Concepts in Action : A Practitioner's Handbook by Bob Williams & Richard Hummelbrunner. Copyright (c) 2010 by the Board of Trustees of the Leland Stanford Jr. University. All rights reserved. Used with the permission of Stanford University Press, www.sup.org.

Social Network Analysis seeks to map, and thus understand, the nature and impact of networks of interconnections. There are many variations but a classic network diagram will look something like this[17]:

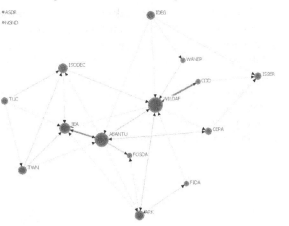

Careful analysis of these patterns reveals a lot about the success and stability of networks and how information or any other resource flows from one part of the network to another.

The analysis generally includes:

- How many links a particular node has to other nodes
- The direction of the flow between the nodes
- The kind of flow between nodes
- The quantity of flow between the nodes

By placing this pattern alongside, say, resource allocation decisions, you can judge whether the right resources are going to the best places within a network.

Systems approaches especially good at changing and managing situations

Cynefin is an approach developed from knowledge management, complexity theory and network theory. It distinguishes between four different patterns that situations display: simple, complicated, complex and chaotic, plus a fifth distinction where the pattern is unclear. The approach identifies management strategies for each of these patterns.

CDE model drawn from Human Systems Dynamics. It explores the way in which framing systems properties as containers (C), differences (D) and exchanges (E) can enable us to understand and influence how complex systems work. A container provides the space within which a situation operates. Containers typically are ideas, physical spaces or groups of people. Small, and the agents are constrained and do not self-organise. Large, and the agents just rattle around the space at random. In between they have the opportunity to self-organise. Differences provide the energy necessary to self-organise. They can be ideological, ethnical, organisational hierarchies, histories, role differentiation and so on. Too small a difference and there is no energy, too big and the situation blows itself apart. Exchanges provide the information or material necessary for the agents to connect with each other. Without that connection, there is no means of expressing difference.

In the CDE model, the relative balance of containers, differences and exchanges determines where a situation lies on the continuum from organised through to self-organising to disorganised. Skilfully used, the model provides insights that enable you to use those elements to influence system change.

And finally — towards multiple methodologies

All of the above approaches are described in more detail in the book *Systems Concepts in Action: A Practitioner's Toolkit* by Richard Hummelbrunner and Bob Williams. A quick search on the internet will bring up many other excellent introductions to these approaches. We have listed a few of them in the Further Reading section of this book.

In this book we have suggested two possible ways of using systems ideas. The majority of the book has focused on applying systems ideas in your own practice. We've taken you through a possible route, well, three actually. This last section has suggested the option of learning and applying entire methodologies or systems approaches. There is a third possibility, that of applying many different systems approaches to a particular wicked problem — a bit of Soft Systems here, a bit of Cynefin there, a dash of CSH within a CDE influenced approach. It's not an approach to be taken lightly, you have to know your systems methods inside out or have access to those that do,

---

[17] Davies, R.J (2009) The Use of Social Network Analysis Tools in the Evaluation of Social Change Communication. Communications for Social Change Consortium.

but if this interests you then the case studies contained in the Gerald Midgley book listed in Further Reading are worth a read.

The final point we want to make is that there is not *the* systems theory; there is not *the* systems approach any more than there is *the* learning theory or *the* management approach. But there is a well-established, diverse field of practice that is discernibly systemic in nature and suited to addressing wicked problems and developing wicked solutions. From this diverse field of practice we have distilled three core features and taken you through a process that uses them. If you've reached this part of the book, you've either followed the age old practice of reading the last chapter first and remain uncertain what this is all about, or you've read the whole thing and are still miraculously with us. But for both of you, our message is the same. Ultimately it doesn't matter whether you adopt or adapt our systems approach or any systems approach. What matters is that you *are* systemic in your thinking and action — indeed your very being.

Where our ideas come from

Standing on the shoulders of giants

Inscription on UK £2 coin

In an infinite universe there's no such thing as a new idea. All authors build on foundations formed by others. This book is no exception. We didn't want to load the main text down with too much theory or systems history, but we cannot finish the book without acknowledging the contribution of two key figures in the systems field: Peter Checkland and C. West Churchman.

Peter Checkland and Soft Systems

In his years as a manager at ICI, a major British plastics company, Peter Checkland became increasingly disillusioned with the application of classic systems engineering ideas to management problems. In particular, he identified that the formal definition of a particular management problem often failed to provide guidance to its resolution.

Checkland's insight was, at the time, revolutionary. Existing systems methods assumed that a given set of inter-relationships would be understood by everyone in roughly the same way. His experience as a manager, however, told him that this was not so; different people within a situation are working to different objectives, based on different perspectives. These differences influence their behaviour and thus the dynamics and their understanding of a situation. Addressing a situation regarded as problematic required an understanding of the multiple perspectives that people brought to that situation.

Subsequently, during the late 1960s, while Professor of Engineering at Lancaster University in the UK, Checkland developed ideas he dubbed 'soft systems' (to contrast with the more deterministic 'hard systems' of systems engineering) as well as the approach known as Soft Systems Methodology. Implicit in this approach is the idea that merely observing a situation and then mapping or modelling it will lead to fewer insights than identifying the different ways a situation can be appreciated through different perspectives and modelling or mapping each of those ways. These conceptual models, each based on a single way of framing or understanding the situation, were not possible 'solutions' but tools that when compared with the rich messiness of the real life situation allowed deeper insights about the situation to be drawn and more robust solutions to be generated.

Soft Systems Methodology heavily influenced the perspective sections of this book. Indeed rich picturing is a soft systems technique.

C. West Churchman and Critical Systems

Churchman was a fascinating character and polymath. He was both a Professor of Business Administration and Professor of Peace and Conflict Studies at University of California, Berkeley. His concerns centred on the ethical decisions taken when constructing systems viewpoints. Indeed, much of his international fame arose from insisting, essentially, that management was not primarily a technical or even social process but an exercise in applied ethics.

According to Churchman, our most critical problem today is understanding the systems we live in. However, it is in the nature of systems to have a continuing perception and deception, an unending reviewing of the world, of the whole system and of its components. These are inseparable from human living (and politics, management, etc.). According to Churchman the main claim to fame of the systems approach is the expansion of our capacity for inquiry. Churchman devised a scheme for the examination ('systemic inquiry') of human system interventions and their design ('planning'), which he called the 'systems approach'.

He concludes his first book on the systems approach with formulating four principles of a deception-perception approach to systems:

I.   "The systems approach begins when first you see the world through the eyes of another."
II.   "The systems approach goes on discovering that every world view is terribly restricted." Or, in Churchman's words (TSA, 231): "Every world view looks only at a component of some other system. For those who think in the large, the 'world' is forever expanding; for those who think in the small, the inner world is forever contracting."
III.   "There are no experts in the systems approach." The public always knows more than any expert (or politician). The problem of the systems approach is to learn what 'everybody' knows. "At the same time, the real expert is still Everyman, stupid, humorous, serious, and comprehensive all at the same time." (TSA, 231-232).
IV.   "The systems approach is not a bad idea."

More profoundly, Churchman believed that our choice of what lies inside a system is essentially an ethical decision. By choosing what lies inside a system you implicitly or even explicitly marginalise what lies outside the system. Thus, Critical Systems is essentially about boundaries. Churchman argued that your choice of what lies inside a system's boundaries depends on your perspective, or more deeply, your values. If these choices are not reflected upon they may well result in exacerbating the very problem you are seeking to address. Indeed it may well cause you to frame the problem in unhelpful ways.[18]

Other important influences

One of Churchman's students, Werner Ulrich, took Churchman's ideas rooted in the school of American Pragmatism and blended them with European schools of thought to produce the Critical Systems Heuristics that form the basis of Level 3 and beyond of this book. Over the past 20 years Gerald Midgley, Michael Jackson and Martin Reynolds have deliberated on, debated and developed Checkland's, Churchman's and Ulrich's ideas. Their fingerprints — admittedly at times somewhat smudged — are all over this book. We take full responsibility for any deviations and misrepresentations of their work and ideas we made in this book. Consequently, we've provided some key references to their work in the next section of this book so that you can read the original texts.

Acknowledgments

Putting aside the formal, technical contributions of Messrs Churchman, Checkland, Ulrich, Midgley, Jackson and Reynolds, many other people have contributed to this book in important ways. In no particular order honourable mentions must go to Patricia Rogers, Richard Hummelbrunner, Jane Davidson, Ricardo Wilson-Grau, Bob Dick, Heather Britt, Elliot Stern, Meg Hargreaves, Gene Bellinger, Jan Noga, Mary McEathron, Judy Oakden, Margo Beth Fleming, Stefanie Krapp, Michael Quinn Patton, Glenda Eoyang, our copy editor Nikki Crutchley of Crucial Corrections, BoJe@nne for her design advice, members of the American Evaluation Association's Systems and

---

18 The following report shows how Churchman applies his systems approach: Churchman, C. W., Nelson, H. G., & Excrete, K. (1977). Value distribution assessment of geothermal development in Lake County, CA. Retrieved from http://www.osti.gov/bridge/servlets/purl/6670871-RBjYQE/6670871.pdf

Evaluation Topical Interest Group, and everyone who's attended one of our workshops over the past decade; especially those workshops that didn't quite go according to plan!

Special mention to Deutsches Evaluierungsinstitut der Entwicklungszusammenarbeit (DEval) in Bonn and the IDRC funded Ecohealth Fieldbuilding Leadership Initiative (FBLI) in South East Asia, which unintentionally but crucially provided the platform upon which this book is built.

Finally dear reader, and now colleague, we'd like to acknowledge your efforts in giving these ideas space in your own minds and activities. We'd like to know how you used the ideas and thoughts about where this book can accommodate those ideas in subsequent versions.

Bob Williams , Wellington
bob@bobwilliams.co.nz or
http://www.bobwilliams.co.nz

Sjon van 't Hof , Amersfoort
sjonvanthof@systemicagency.org or
http://www.systemicagency.org

Further reading

Systems approaches in general

Jackson, Michael C. 2003. *Systems thinking: Creative holism for managers*. New York: Wiley.

Midgley, Gerald. 2000. *Systemic intervention: Philosophy, methodology, and practice*. New York: Kluwer Academic/Plenum.

Ramage, Magnus & Karen Shipp. 2009. *Systems thinkers*. London: Springer.

Reynolds, Martin & Sue Holwell (Eds.).2010. *Systems approaches to managing change: A practical guide*. London: Springer.

Williams, Bob & Richard Hummelbrunner. 2011. *Systems concepts in action: A Practitioner's Toolkit*. Stanford: Stanford University Press.

Systems approaches used in this book

Inter-relationships:
The Open University in the UK provides some excellent insights and advice about Rich Pictures. This website contains a lot of valuable advice, much of which informed this book:

http://systems.open.ac.uk/materials/T552/pages/rich/rich.html.

http://systems.open.ac.uk/materials/T552/pages/rich/rp-miners.html

Perspectives:
Checkland, Peter & Jim Scholes. 1999. *Soft systems methodology in action*. New York: John Wiley and Sons.

Checkland, P. 2000. Soft systems methodology: a thirty year retrospective. *Systems Research*, *17*.
http://citeseerx.ist.psu.edu/viewdoc/download?doi=10.1.1.133.7381&rep=rep1&type=pdf

Boundaries:
Reynolds, Martin.2007. Evaluation based on critical systems heuristics. In *Using systems concepts in evaluation: An expert anthology* (pp. 101–122). Point Reyes CA, USA: EdgePress. http://oro.open.ac.uk/3464/1/Evaluation_CSH_-_Reynolds.pdf

Reynolds, Martin. 2010. *Evaluation and stakeholding development*. Presented at the 9th European Evaluation Society International Conference, Prague, Czech Republic.
http://oro.open.ac.uk/26778/1/EES_Prague10_paperMR.pdf

Ulrich, W. 2005. *A brief introduction to critical systems heuristics*
.http://projects.kmi.open.ac.uk/ecosensus/publications/ulrich_csh_intro.pdf

Williams, Bob & Martin Reynolds. 2012. Systems thinking for equity-focused evaluations. In *Evaluation for equitable development results* (pp. 115–141). New York: UNICEF.
http://mymande.org/sites/default/files/Evaluation_for_equitable_results.zip.

Specific systems methodologies and methods

There are hundreds of books and websites describing specific systems methods and methodologies. Below are some references and websites we have found useful. All URLs were checked in February 2014.

Williams, Bob & Richard Hummelbrunner. 2011. *Systems concepts in action: A Practitioner's Toolkit*. Stanford: Stanford University Press. This book provides a general overview of a dozen or so systems methods and methodologies. It is available as a book.

Social Network Analysis:

Hanneman, Robert A. & Mark Riddle. 2005. *Introduction to social network methods*. Riverside: University of California.

International Network for Social Network Analysis: http://www.insna.org

System Dynamics:

Sterman, John D. 2000. *Business dynamics: Systems thinking and modelling for a complex world*. Boston: Irwin/McGraw-Hill.

System Dynamics Society: http://www.systemdynamics.org

Complex Adaptive Systems:

Eoyang, Glenda. 1997. *Coping with chaos: Seven simple tools*. Circle Pines, MN: Lagumo.

Brenda Zimmerman, Curt Lindberg, & Paul Plsek (1990/2009) *A complexity science primer: What is complexity science and why should I learn about it?* An adapted version is available here: http://aidontheedge.files.wordpress.com/2009/11/complexity-science-primer.doc

Ramalingham, Ben 2013. *Aid on the edge of chaos: Rethinking international cooperation in a complex world*. Oxford University Press.

Cynefin

Cognitive Edge Web site. http://www.cognitive-edge.com/.▮

Kurtz, Cynthia F., and David J. Snowden. 2003. The new dynamics of strategy: Sense-making in a complex and complicated world. *IBM Journal of Research and Development 42(3) 462–483.*▮

Patton, Michael Q. 2010. *Developmental evaluation*. New York: Guilford Press.

Snowden, David. J., and Mary E. Boone. 2007. *A leader's framework for decision-making*. Harvard Business Review. November: 69–76.

Human Systems Dynamics:

Human Systems Dynamics Institute *http://www.hsdinstitute.org*

Soft Systems:

Checkland, Peter B. & John. Poulter. 2006. *Learning for action: A short definitive account of soft systems methodology and its use for practitioners, teachers and students*. Chichester, NY: Wiley.

Williams B. No date. *Soft Systems Methodology*

http://www.bobwilliams.co.nz/Systems_Resources_files/ssm.pdf

Activity Systems:

Center for Research on Activity Development and Learning (CRADLE), University of Helsinki http://www.helsinki.fi/cradle/

Viable Systems:

Tepe, Susanne & Tim Haslett. 2002. Occupational Health and Safety Systems, Corporate Governance and Viable Systems Diagnosis: An Action Research Approach. *Systemic Practice and Action Research, 15(6)*, December2002.

Walker, Jon. 2006. *The Viable System Model*. Version 3.0. http://www.esrad.org.uk/resources/vsmg_3/screen.php?page=home

Jargon buster

Words don't have definitions, only uses.

'Thinking with Concepts' : John Wilson

We've tried hard to avoid too much systems jargon in this book, but sometimes there was no alternative. In any case as a systems thinker you'll benefit from learning the language of the trade. Here's a list of words that may have been new to you or used in unfamiliar ways. In some cases the words are used in different ways even within the systems field, and we felt it important that you are clear how we are using them.

Agent A component of a situation. It could be people or things. Often the nodes of network relationships.

Boundary Marks an important distinction between two features of a situation. It determines what is 'in' or what is 'out', what's important or valid and what is unimportant or invalid; what is included and what is marginalised.

Boundary Critique The means by which you consider the implications of particular boundary decisions.

Boundary Decision The choice of where to place a boundary.

Complex situations Situations whose behaviour is knowable only after the fact; uncertain and unpredictable.

Complicated situations Situations whose behaviour is knowable but not necessarily know, and once known is relatively predictable.

Context Something that affects how a situation behaves but over which that situation has little influence or control. Often used to mean the same thing as 'environment' but generally is a bit more abstract and conceptual. History is often an important aspect of context.

Critical Systems Heuristic A heuristic for the systemic inquiry of intervention designs, which helps you structure the questions that enable you to find out whether the intervention is justified or not.

Dynamic How agents inter-relate and the consequences of those inter-relationships over time.

Environmental fallacy Acceptance of partial solution to wider systemic problem by not thinking through the negative (systemic) consequences of action proposals.

Feedback The phenomenon where an output of a process becomes the input of the same process.

Framing Collection of perspectives that help you make sense of a situation in a particular way. 'Human rights' or 'Entertainment' are examples of framings.

Guarantor: A person or mechanism that ensures that the expertise and knowledge used is appropriate and effective.

Heuristic A heuristic is a framework for structuring the questions that enable you to find out the things you need to know. In this book the heuristics are contained within a matrix of 12 inter-related design categories.

Inter-Relationship Connections between components or agents within a situation.

Marginalisation In boundary setting, an aspect of a situation is marginalised if it is considered unimportant.

Network A set of inter-relationships between objects or agents.

Object A component of a situation. It could be people or things. Often the nodes of network relationships.

Output What a process directly produces.

Pattern A set of repeated behaviours.

Perspective Values, assumptions and viewpoints that stakeholders bring to and make sense of a situation.

Problem A situation that is of some concern or that contains issues that need addressing.

Rich Picture A graphic means of displaying key features of a situation that is unstructured and unfettered by preconceived views and ideas. Used extensively in soft systems approaches.

Simple situations Situations whose behaviour is wholly known and predictable.

Situation The set of circumstances that are of interest to us and on which we intend to apply systems concepts.

Situation of interest In systems language, a state of affairs that is of interest to you that you wish to explore further or intervene in.

Stake Motivations, worldviews and other factors that could benefit from or be at risk because of the situation, and influence the behaviour or perspectives of stakeholders.

Stakeholder Someone or something that can affect or be affected by a situation or any action to address a situation.

Stakeholding An issue, or set of issues that are the consequence of a particular stakeholder's relationship with his or her stakes in the situation of interest.

Sweeping in A critical systems concept that implies taking in as many aspects of the situation as deemed relevant to addressing the situation of interest.

System A much disputed concept that within this book is used to describe an aspect of a situation that we choose to observe and describe using systems concepts.

Systemic The process of thinking or applying ideas drawn from the systems field.

Systems Field An approach to inquiry and design that comprises a wide range of different methodologies, methods and techniques that we believe has a distinctive approach to inter-relationships, perspectives and boundaries.

Systems Thinking A means of understanding the world using systems concepts.

Transformation Achieving a result that has higher value or meaning.

Unfolding A critical systems concept that requires thinking through the implications of design choices made in one design category for design aspects in the same or other categories.

Valuation Assigning value or meaning or purpose, e.g., to design aspects.

Value mapping Combines unfolding 'is-ought' using CSH scheme, including stakeholding entrenchment/development.

Worldview A set of values and attitudes that influence how you engage with a situation.

Figure on next page: One-page 'poster' summary of the worked case of *making smallholder irrigation sustainable* using a systems approach at level three of this book.

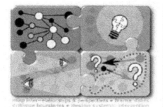

Making smallholder irrigation sustainable:

a case illustrating the systems approach to complex problems using **Wicked Solutions**

1. Problem identification

Problem: Failure of making pump-based lift irrigation sustainable. **Background:** Sahel (Senegal-Chad), 200-600 mm rainfall. Droughts, climate change. Major rivers: Senegal, Gambia, Niger, Mouhoun, Hadejia, Logone, Chari. Decades of development efforts to introduce diesel-powered lift irrigation to fight food insecurity.

2. Rich picture

Maps inter-relationships (incl. processes), key stake-holders and stakes (values, motivations, assumptions). Place post-its on big sheet of paper, arrange, and draw unartistically. Also maps context and resources.

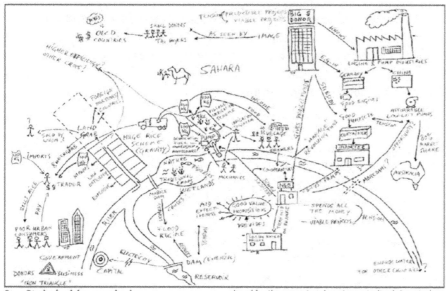

3. Stakeholder analysis

Carries out influence mapping by looking at the relative importance of + and –ive impacts (active and passive)

Stakeholder roles	... have an effect on	... are affected by	Importance
Big overseas donors	the choices and the right of irrigation projects; solve chronic poverty	tax payers; overseas governments; exit quotas	++
NGOs	selection of pumps	donor money flow; conscious about project design logic	+
Irrigation expert	functioning/operation of village irrigation scheme	short term practicalities	+
Farmers	financial sustainability of village irrigation scheme	poverty, hunger; unpredictable river flow; conscious about project design logic	++
Village leaders	irrigation scheme management	farmers' willingness to pay for irrigation	+
National or local government	project planning and design; river basin management; river flow (dam regulation); health & agricultural policy	local interest groups; voters; donors/landlords, aid	+
Pump importers & dealers	the type of pumping equipment available	margins; device performances; manufacturers; price of rice; flow of income	+
Rice consumers	rice imports		+

4. Stake identification

Identifies stakes of key stakeholders with regard to purpose and its definition, resources and their control, knowledge and its acknowledgment, and legitimacy or fairness of, or relevance to the intervention.

Stakeholder roles	Stakes	Importance
Big overseas donors	Sustainable projects; Reducing hunger	++
NGOs	Continuous flow of projects; NGO mission	+
Irrigation expert	Efficient implementation	+
Farmers	Growing enough food for family; Access to pumps; Farm income; Sustainable projects	++
Village leaders	Best possible deal for the village; Leadership	+
National or Local Government	National food production	+
Private sector importers & service providers	Profit, turnover, market share; Sustainable projects	++
Rice consumers	Low food prices	+

5. Framings

Use the key stakes to frame your intervention in a general way. Three complementary framings are often enough.

Framings		
Food production	Income generation	Market for pumps

6. Rich picture exploration

Summarizes key ideas from the rich picture, e.g. on

Pump irrigation: The farmers and their families live in villages along the river. They work in association to grow rice in so/called village irrigation schemes, but they are not an egalitarian bunch. A key question is what value can be produced for the poorest and most marginalized. A central pump lifts the water from the river into the canals. The pump costs money for depreciation, fuel, financing, and maintenance.

Pump origin: In the right part of the rich picture we see equipment of Western or Asian origin. The latter is a fraction of the cost of the former, but perhaps less reliable. Yet, it works well in Asia: millions of irrigation smallholders would not have been there without them. Moreover, affordable pumps of the right design from China have an 80% market share in the Australian market, where they are combined with Western engines. *For several other explanations consult the book.*

7. Outline of the ideal situation

In 5 or 10 years from now a steadily growing number of farmer groups ought to be in a position to hire or hire-purchase optimized pumpsets at fair prices from an efficient private sector, which seeks to cover as many farmers as possible and which provides them with additional services for maintenance and input supply. This will centralize and streamline the problems of pump procurement and maintenance and will provide farmers with the necessary incentives to pay for the pumpsets. None of this will be possible without an optimized value proposition.

8. Boundary critique

This is a systemic inquiry into the boundary choices that define the why of "is" and how of "ought" using questions based on a twelve-category heuristic. The twelve categories are: Beneficiaries, **Purpose**, Measures of performance, Decision makers, **Resources**, Environment, Designers/planners, **Knowledge**, Guarantor, Witnesses,

Legitimacy, and world View. Questions based on these categories are applied to both "is" and "ought". The answers (or "boundary choices") to these questions provide the elements needed for outlining a possible intervention design (see book).

9. Systemic intervention design

Overview   Use post-it's for a full overview of the critique

Summary   Summarize the key points of the "ought" situation for the questions relating to purpose, resources, knowledge and legitimacy:

Purpose The key transformation in the 'ought' mode is to lift the constraints on equipment renewal, food production, and income generation at a large enough scale for achieving self sustaining growth of a responsive private sector serving smallholder farmers empowered to exercise effective demand in a mutually beneficial relationship with that private sector.

'Ought' critique of 'is' The goal of food security may be commendable, but targeting farmers directly is not sustainable. Target group farmers are not served well, while non-target group farmers are not served at all. The private sector provides some services, but these services are far from optimized. Special attention ought to be paid to the payment arrangements. Ideally, these are embedded in the rural services. Farm households need cash income as well as food. Co-operative development training maintenance. Indicators for sustainability are lacking.

'Is' critique of 'ought' Care should be taken not to pamper the private sector with aid funds. Or else, the project mode of aid delivery directly to (poor) farm households in the old situation may be preferable, provided training is improved. The establishment of better and cheaper rural services is not an easy task. In one generation crop marketing at remote rural areas is difficult. In the end it may be just as difficult to create a sustainable solution with private sector involvement as without.

Resources In our 'ought' mode we believe the key decisions are still taken by donors and development organizations, but a stronger role will be available much earlier in the programme for those stakeholders that will determine ultimate sustainability and effectiveness, viz. the farmers and the private sector.

'Ought' critique of 'is' & 'is' critique of 'ought'

Knowledge In the 'ought' mode the value proposition of the intervention is connected by bringing in business expertise for enterprise development and technical and commercial expertise for pump selection and procurement.

'Ought' critique of 'is' & 'is' critique of 'ought'

Legitimacy In the 'ought' model of development, donors acknowledge that they can no longer support risk-avoiding interventions that entail low sustainability.

'Ought' critique of 'is' & 'is' critique of 'ought'

Design   The final design is a synthesis of the ideas generated by the critique. To make the design practical and feasible some additional ideas had to be added. To repeat ourselves, this is our idea of what might be feasible or right.

Purpose and beneficiaries The purpose is to lift the constraints on equipment renewal, food production, and income generation by achieving self sustaining growth of a responsive private sector. The direct beneficiary is the private sector with the smallholder irrigation farmers as its clients. The private sector beneficiaries are: a. international equipment sellers from Europe (engines) and Asia (pumping equipment), b. national equipment importers in Sahelian countries, c. local pump rental and credit systems to serve the farmers, and other local enterprises to provide various services to farmers, e.g. for input supply, pump maintenance and repair, transport and marketing.

Resources and decision-making A new actor will be established by the donor to provide the above chain of private sector beneficiaries with the necessary co-ordination to become responsive to the farmer needs and make a fair profit serving them. This new coordination centre (CC) for smallholder irrigation development will be a social enterprise. Once it will have achieved a certain scale of operations it will no longer need external support or subsidies. Initially the CC will have to invest in confidence building between the various stakeholders. The CC will also channel considerable financial resources in the form of low interest loans towards capital development of pumping equipment. To do so effectively it will help establish and supervise effective local pump rental and credit businesses. These local pump rental businesses will develop and manage a network of farmer groups and small local enterprises to serve these farmers. Reasonable assurances must be sought from government with regard to ...

Knowledge and guarantor During the initial phase, the CC will be an important provider of knowledge. Knowledge for the design and procurement of Asian pumping equipment (cost efficiency, reliability), knowledge for ensuring adequate involvement of the private sector (incentives/loans, business plans, competitive price formation), and knowledge to establish payment arrangements.

Legitimacy and worldview The intervention is designed to address a deep concern about the failure of making pump-based, smallholder irrigation for food production along Sahelian rivers sustainable. In the old set-up everybody loses: Western tax payers, Sahelian farmers, donors, and various private sector actors ...

10. Final check

You now have a solid start to addressing your wicked problem with a wicked solution. During implementation you will need to ensure you stay focused and redesign when necessary. A systemic view, a systemic approach, is always incomplete. Action creates further information and further insights. It's a good idea to keep an eye on the following issues: 1. How is the 'rich picture' looking? Do you want to add to it? 2. How do any new ways of framing the situation improve your understanding and strategies? 3. What new boundary issues have arisen?

About the authors

Bob Williams

Bob has been using systems concepts in his work for over 30 years. He was originally trained as an ecologist — one of the earliest 'systems' disciplines — and spent four years with the Systems Group at the Open University in the United Kingdom. He is well versed in a variety of different systems methods, including relatively 'old' approaches, such as system dynamics and soft systems methodology, as well as relatively new ones, such as complex adaptive systems, critical systems and activity theory.

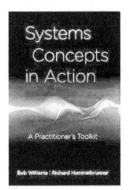

For the past few years Bob has been exploring how to adapt systems ideas and systems methods into the practice of evaluating and redesigning complex social programmes. In particular, he is interested in how systems concepts can be applied to methods of inquiry, analysis and design that do not originate in the systems field. In other words, how to make more 'systemic' the methods you are familiar with and use expertly in your own work rather than learn an entirely new bunch of methods; hence, this book. In 2014 he received the Lazarsfeld Award of the American Evaluation Association (AEA) for contributions to "fruitful debates on the assumptions, goals and practices of evaluation."

But if you are interested in systems methods then his book with Richard Hummelbrunner, Systems Concepts in Action: A Practitioner's Toolkit describes twenty of them (see Further Reading).

bob@bobwilliams.co.nz

http://www.bobwilliams.co.nz

Sjon van 't Hof

Sjon got acquainted with systems thinking while working at the Royal Tropical Institute in Amsterdam. First he was introduced to multi-stakeholder learning in agricultural innovation systems (RAAKS or Rapid Appraisal of Agricultural Knowledge Systems) and a few years afterwards to the use of monitoring and evaluation to facilitate learning in rural development. He is convinced that the complexity of international development projects and programmes often goes unrecognised while at the same time the systems tools needed to deal with complexity issues are unknown, ignored or considered impractical. Only systemic agency can help achieve aid effectiveness.

He has a background in tropical agriculture (BSc) and irrigation engineering (MSc, Cranfield University). In the early 1980s he worked as a land use planning officer in Zambia, and in the late 1980s and early 1990s as an irrigation engineer for UNICEF in Timbuktu. In more recent years he has carried out missions in Bangladesh, Burkina Faso, Cameroon, Chad, Ghana, India, China, Kenya, Mauritania and Niger. The common thread in his work is understanding and strengthening the smallholder perspective in agricultural development efforts.

sjonvanthof@systemicagency.org

http://www.systemicagency.org

CPSIA information can be obtained
at www.ICGtesting.com
Printed in the USA
LVHW061817210820
663839LV00009B/372

9 781326 512293